This book is gratefully dedicated to William Humbert, the incredibly gifted artist who produced the creative illustrations in these pages, and whose personal life exemplifies the training principles and practices presented in the text.

Contents

Acknowledgments

It is a great privilege to acknowledge the literary leadership of Ted Miller, Martin Barnard, Wendy McLaughlin, Leigh LaHood, and the many other professionals at Human Kinetics who made this book possible. Special thanks to Marsha Young for preparing the text, to William Humbert for illustrating the manuscript, and to Tom Roberts for the flawless photographs. I am most appreciative of my colleagues at Nautilus, Jim Teatum, Doug Werner, Mark Urlage, and Mike Burney; at the South Shore YMCA, Ralph Yohe, Mary Hurley, Bill Johnson, Rita LaRosa Loud, Tracy D'Arpino, Gayle Laing, Cindy Long, Cheryl Rosa, and Lynne Powers; and at Navy Fitness, Kelly Powell and James Baker. My sincere gratitude to my exercise models Olivia Chamberland, Ryan Donnelly, Scott Hutchinson, and Taelese Piers. Finally, I am most thankful for my wife, Claudia, and God's grace for enabling me to complete the second edition of *Building Strength & Stamina*.

Introduction

You already know that physical fitness is an essential component of a healthy and satisfying lifestyle. Plus, you really want exercise to occupy a prominent place in your daily schedule. However, because so many books, videos, magazines, and training tips are available, it can be confusing to determine which activities to do and how to perform them properly. That's where this book can help. *Building Strength & Stamina, Second Edition,* provides all the information needed to develop high levels of muscular strength, cardiovascular endurance, and joint flexibility for greater overall physical fitness than may have seemed possible. In fact, this is one of the few books that place almost equal emphasis on both strength and endurance exercise.

The book is set up in four parts: learning to integrate strength and endurance training into workouts; strength logistics and basic exercises; endurance logistics, equipment, and routines; and finally, workout programs. This way you'll know exactly what you're getting into and you can apply that knowledge to your own individualized workout, be it a two- or six-month program.

The exercise programs presented in this book are highly productive, and you will achieve excellent results in relatively short periods. What's more, the programs are easy to understand, simple to implement, and safe to perform. The well-researched principles for improving strength and endurance are presented clearly and concisely, with emphasis on practical application at either a fitness center or in the home. To facilitate productive and progressive exercise experiences, you may follow the two-month sample training programs for both muscular and cardiovascular fitness. These programs are set up for people of all ages and fitness levels. If you're interested in increasing your fitness level after the initial two-month program, the book provides six-month sample training programs as well.

This edition of *Building Strength & Stamina* also includes information from new studies of high-intensity strength training and circuit strength training. These procedures are more advanced approaches to strength and muscle development that are extremely effective yet exceptionally time-efficient. Ten of the professional football teams in the National Football League currently train in a similar manner, typically performing two or three 45- to 60-minute strength workouts per week. You should be pleasantly surprised by the excellent results attained from these high-effort but short-duration strength training techniques. Likewise, more attention is given to advanced forms of endurance exercise to maximize cardiovascular fitness. You will learn how to enhance your aerobic capacity through interesting and productive exercise programs such as interval training, cross-training, and fartlek training.

Undoubtedly, the major addition to the second edition of *Building Strength & Stamina* is the attention given to free weight training. Equal emphasis is placed on the 30 machine exercises and the 27 free weight exercises that address all of the major muscle groups. When performed properly and in accordance with the specific strength training principles presented in the preceding chapters, these precisely explained and clearly illustrated strength exercises should maximize your muscle-building potential. The recommended exercises and workout protocols represent the most effective and efficient means of safely and successfully achieving higher levels of strength fitness.

Combining the carefully designed strength, endurance, and flexibility components into a comprehensive conditioning program should be a satisfying process with reinforcing results. Just as important, the highly productive yet relatively brief training sessions should facilitate workout scheduling and compliance for an exercise program that can keep you fit for a lifetime. Specifically, our beginning research participants typically increase their strength by about 50 percent after just two months of standard training. During that same time period, women generally add one to two pounds of muscle, and men generally gain three to four pounds of muscle. Significantly, our studies with already fit, advanced exercisers show approximately 20 percent greater strength and one to two pounds more muscle after two months of high-intensity training.

We have learned from our research studies that you can successfully combine strength training and endurance exercise with no negative effects on strength or muscle development. Much to our surprise, we have also discovered that you can enhance normal strength gains by up to 20 percent when you concurrently perform strength training and stretching exercise. This trio of exercise activities (strength, stretching, and endurance) assures a comprehensive approach to physical fitness, resulting in a strong and flexible musculoskeletal system and a functional cardiovascular system.

The key to enhancing overall physical fitness is training technique. How you perform each exercise is unquestionably the most important factor in your fitness development. That is why *Building Strength & Stamina* places so much emphasis on exercise performance, with special attention to the technical aspects of movement patterns, movement range, movement speed, and biomechanical considerations. The exercises are presented clearly and concisely so that you'll know you're doing them correctly. Doing them is up to you, but this book provides all the tools you need to achieve your fitness goals safely, effectively, and efficiently.

Integrating Strength and Endurance

Did you know that less than 10 percent of American adults exercise enough to gain measurable fitness benefits?[1] As you begin your fitness regimen, think about the reasons you want to become more physically fit. Are you a runner who wants a stronger upper body? How about a tennis player trying to stay in shape during the off-season? Or are you an average man or woman seeking better posture, confidence, and strength in your appearance and lifestyle? These goals will be your motivation and will guide your workouts every day, so it is important to know what you want out of an exercise program.

Strength and Endurance Exercise

If you want to get into shape for better sport performance, keep in mind that one-dimensional, sport-specific training often prevents athletes from developing well-balanced fitness. Football players stress strength and power exercises but may neglect aerobic conditioning. Distance runners emphasize endurance training but may pay little attention to strength development.

Building Strength & Stamina, Second Edition, incorporates a complete training program, combining muscle-strengthening exercises with aerobic activity for cardiovascular enhancement. By following this training program, you can achieve both better general fitness and superior sport conditioning.

Exercising for Strength

The primary purpose of strength exercise is to improve muscle function. Resistance exercise will make you feel like the high-performance person you'd like to be. It will also develop stronger bones, tendons, and ligaments, enabling you to perform better in all physical activities. In addition, strength exercise reduces your risk of medical problems, including low back pain, illnesses such as diabetes, and degenerative problems such as osteoporosis.

While it is obvious that fit muscles enhance personal appearance, strength training has another great advantage you may not be aware of. If you struggle with keeping your weight down, this is the activity for you! Regular strength training not only increases your daily energy expenditure, but it also boosts your resting metabolism.[2] People who perform strength exercise burn more calories all day long, making it easier to attain and maintain their desirable body weight.

Exercising for Endurance

The primary purpose of endurance exercise is to strengthen the cardiovascular system. This includes the heart, lungs, and blood vessels. Some of the more obvious outcomes of cardiovascular conditioning include a lower resting heart rate, reduced resting blood pressure, improved exercise performance, and faster physical recovery after exercise of any kind.

Aerobic fitness and cardiovascular health are closely related. The same aerobic adaptations that produce better endurance performance also reduce the risk of coronary artery disease, stroke, and other cardiovascular illnesses. When combined with strength exercise, endurance activity enables the muscles to use energy more efficiently. And endurance training effectively burns extra calories, reducing body fat in the process.

Understanding Realistic Expectations

In addition to learning the benefits of strength and endurance training, you need to understand how inherited physical factors influence fitness potential. Such knowledge enables you to establish realistic training goals and to follow sensible exercise guidelines. No matter who you are, you can become more fit, but we all have certain genetic limitations we need to accept.

Strength Potential

We all have the ability to increase our muscle size and strength within certain limits. Regardless of gender or age, you can improve your muscular fitness through well-designed strength training programs. You may be surprised to learn, however, that age, gender, and body build all affect your potential for strength development.

Age

People often believe that boys and girls under 15 years are too young and men and women 55 years and older are too old to benefit from strength training. In fact, people of all ages can increase their muscle size and strength through a basic program of resistance exercise.

As a case in point, we recently evaluated more than 400 people of all ages who performed eight weeks of standard Nautilus exercise.[3] All of the program participants significantly increased their lean (muscle) weight. The youths (average age of 12 years) added four pounds of lean weight, the younger adults (average age of 45 years) added three pounds of lean weight, and the seniors (average age of 65 years) added three pounds of lean weight.

Of course, part of the youths' gain in lean weight was due to normal growth processes. But notice that the seniors increased their muscle mass as much as the younger adults. These results are similar to other studies on strength exercise by seniors and indicate that older adults can build muscle tissue at the same rate as younger adults.[4,5]

Likewise, both the senior and younger adult participants increased their strength performance by 50 to 60 percent over the eight-week training period. The youth participants showed a higher rate of strength performance (60 to 75 percent over the same training duration), which, like their greater lean weight gain, was probably due to normal maturation processes.[6,7]

Some people may question the advisability of regular resistance exercise for youths and seniors. However, it is the best way to build strong muscles and bones, which are so important for these age groups. Properly performed strength training is a safe and productive form of exercise for people of all ages. All of the youth, adult, and senior participants in this study remained injury-free throughout the eight-week exercise program.

Gender

Who says women can't lift? Obviously, the average man is larger and stronger than the average woman, and males do have more muscle mass than females. This has led many people to believe that women are inherently weak and so can benefit little from a program of strength exercise. When analyzed on a pound-for-pound basis, however, men and women are very similar in their strength capacities.

For example, we compared leg (quadriceps) strength in over 900 trained men and women.[8] As illustrated in table 1.1, the men appeared to be 50 percent stronger than the women (10 leg extensions with 119 pounds from men versus 10 leg extensions with 79 pounds for women). But when we accounted for body weight differences, the strength quotients were similar (62 percent for men versus 55 percent for women). Furthermore, when we considered that men are genetically programmed for more muscle and less fat than women, the final results were almost identical. When evaluated on a pound-for-pound basis, both the larger-framed men and the smaller-framed women performed 10 leg extensions with about 75 percent of their lean body weight. So men and women have similar levels of leg (quadriceps) strength when fairly evaluated on a lean weight basis.

Other studies involving hundreds of men and women have shown similar gains in muscle size and strength by both genders after several weeks of resistance training.[3] It is clear that men and women have comparable lean weight strength and that they can benefit equally from sensible strength training.

As you can see, no matter what your age or gender, you can achieve significant increases in both muscle size and strength through properly performed strength training.

Body Build

Generally speaking, the four basic body types are ectomorphic, mesomorphic, endomorphic, and endomesomorphic (see figure 1.1).

Table 1.1	Quadriceps Strength for Men and Women	
	Men	**Women**
Age (years)	43	42
Body weight (lb.)	191	143
10-rep maximum (lb.)	119	79
Strength quotient (body weight)	62%	55%
Strength quotient (lean body weight)	74%	73%

1. Ectomorphs—A linear appearance characterizes the ectomorphic physique. Ectomorphs have relatively low amounts of muscle and fat. They are typically light in body weight and are best suited for endurance activities such as distance running.

2. Mesomorphs—The mesomorphic physique is rectangular in appearance. Mesomorphs have relatively high amounts of muscle and relatively low amounts of fat. They are typically medium in body weight and are best suited for strength activities such as wrestling and gymnastics.

3. Endomorphs—The endomorphic physique looks more rounded than the others. Endomorphs have relatively low amounts of muscle but relatively high amounts of fat. A variation is the endomesomorph, who has relatively high amounts of both muscle and fat.

4. Endomesomorphs—Endomesomorphs are typically heavy for their heights and are best suited for power activities, such as football, in which large size is an advantage.

Although mesomorphs have the greatest potential to develop muscular physiques, ectomorphs and endomorphs can also add significant amounts of muscle through sensible strength training. Ectomorphs typically achieve more muscular physiques when they increase their daily consumption of nutritious foods, with attention to sufficient protein and complex carbohydrates. Endomorphs and endomesomorphs may benefit from a nutrition program that emphasizes a low-fat, moderate-calorie diet.

Endurance Potential

As with strength conditioning, everyone has the potential to improve cardiovascular endurance. In addition to age, gender, body build, and muscle fiber type, cardiovascular endurance is related to the ventilation capacity of the lungs, the pumping capacity of the heart, the distribution capacity of the blood vessels, and blood volume (the amount of blood within the circulatory system). All of these factors work together to supply your tissues with oxygen. The amount of oxygen needed for basic life processes is relatively small, but vigorous physical activity greatly increases the oxygen needs of your muscles.

Heart and Lung Capacity

When endurance athletes perform high-level aerobic exercise, their lungs may move more than 150 liters of air a minute, and their hearts may pump up to 40 liters of blood a minute.[9,10] Relative to their body size, endurance athletes have larger lungs, hearts, and arteries than average individuals. They also have more blood vessels and greater blood volume than untrained people. Although endurance training can increase the ability of the muscles to use oxygen, its effect on the size of the heart and blood vessels is not fully understood.[11] Most likely, outstanding endurance athletes are genetically endowed with exceptionally effective cardiovascular systems as well as with favorable muscle physiology.

Age

During your growth years, normal development increases the capacity of your cardiovascular system. However, once you reach adulthood, cardiovascular endurance gradually declines. One reason for this decline is that maximum heart rate steadily decreases with age, and this reduces the pumping capacity of your heart. As

■ **Figure 1.1** Various body types.

a rule, your maximum heart rate lowers about 10 beats a minute every decade. Even so, it is possible for those who haven't been exercising to improve their cardiovascular fitness at any age and for those who do exercise regularly to maintain high levels of aerobic endurance throughout their midlife years.[12]

Gender

Men typically perform better than women in endurance activities, such as distance running, cycling, and triathlons. This performance advantage is probably due to body composition differences between men and women. Male athletes generally have a higher percentage of lean weight and a lower percentage of fat weight than female athletes. Men probably do not have inherently superior cardiovascular systems compared with women. Endurance exercise seems to produce the same physiological adaptations in men and women, and both benefit from regular aerobic activity.

Body Build and Composition

Lower body weight is clearly an advantage for endurance activities, one reason almost all successful marathon runners have ectomorphic physiques. Closely related to body build is body composition—the ratio of fat weight to lean weight, expressed as percent body fat. At a given body weight, people with a lower percentage of fat weight and a higher percentage of lean weight have an advantage in endurance performance. One way to increase your aerobic ability is to achieve a lower percentage of body fat through endurance exercise, strength training, and proper diet.

Muscle Fiber Types

The oxygen-receiving capacity of the muscles affects endurance potential as much as the oxygen-delivering capacity of the cardiovascular system. However, not all muscle fibers utilize oxygen in the same way. Slow-twitch muscle fibers use oxygen more efficiently and resist fatigue better than fast-twitch fibers. Slow-twitch muscle fibers are best suited to endurance exercise, while fast-twitch muscle fibers are best suited to brief bouts of strength exercise.

Summary

Strength exercise improves muscular fitness. A strong musculoskeletal system increases physical performance, reduces risk of injury, and enhances appearance. Certain genetic characteristics, however, influence your strength potential.

Fortunately, men and women of all ages can improve their muscle strength through a progressive program of resistance exercise. Even if you do not make a major change in your body build as a result of strength training, you will still reap major fitness benefits. Stronger muscles, bones, tendons, and ligaments increase your ability to perform physical activity and decrease the risk of musculoskeletal injuries and degenerative diseases. Youths, adults, and seniors all benefit from systematic strength exercise. This is good news because muscle strength is a key factor for overall health and fitness.

Likewise, aerobic exercise improves cardiovascular fitness. An efficient cardiovascular system benefits both physical performance and health. Even though factors such as age and basic body build influence endurance potential, people of all ages can enhance cardiovascular endurance through a regular program of aerobic activity.

People who are overweight generally avoid aerobic activities because they find less satisfaction and success in endurance exercise than strength training. But overweight and heavily muscled people should keep in mind that endurance exercise is an excellent way to burn extra calories. Endurance exercise also provides extra protection against heart disease.

Just as a well-maintained engine and fuel system keep an automobile running well, tuned-up muscular and cardiovascular systems will improve your physical strength and endurance. A combination of strength and endurance fitness will increase your energy level, make you feel and look better, and help you stay healthy longer—all of which will enhance your quality of life. Chapters 2-13 of this book will help you design effective and efficient strength and endurance exercise programs, enabling you to develop high levels of muscular and cardiovascular fitness.

Training for Muscular Strength

You're ready to start strength training. What specific benefits can you expect from the program? How does providing varied amounts of resistance increase your strength and build your muscles? Are certain types of exercises better than others?

As you're about to find out, there's a lot more to strength training than just picking up a dumbbell at the gym and doing 15 reps of biceps curls. A carefully planned regimen, proper technique, and thorough anatomical understanding will give you maximum results.[1] So next time you go to the gym to do so many reps of an exercise, you'll know what to do and how to do it, what resistance level to use, and how it is affecting your individual muscle groups.

Benefits of Strength Training

The primary effect of strength training is an increase in both the strength and the size of muscles. The major muscle groups affected are identified in figure 2.1. But strength training also benefits bones, tendons, ligaments, and digestive and cardio-vascular systems. Regular strength training also reduces the risk of various injuries and illnesses.

In addition to the obvious benefits of increased muscle strength, muscle mass, and muscle endurance, there are many other reasons you should make sensible strength exercise a key part of your lifestyle:

1. Joint flexibility. Properly performed strength training works the exercised muscles through their full range of motion. Keep in mind that muscles act in pairs to flex and extend the joints. For example, when the elbow joint is fully flexed, the biceps muscle is in a shortened (contracted) position and the opposing triceps muscle is in a lengthened (stretched) position, and vice versa, when the joint is fully extended. By performing full-range exercises for all of the major muscle groups, you will enhance your joint flexibility as well as muscle strength.[2,3]

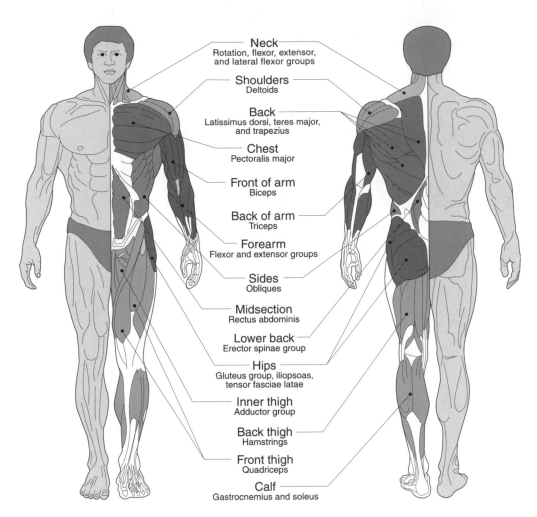

Figure 2.1   Major muscle groups of the human anatomy.

2.   Body composition. Body composition refers to the relative amounts of fat tissue and lean tissue in our bodies and is usually expressed as percent body fat. For example, a 100-pound woman who has 25 percent body fat has 25 pounds of fat weight and 75 pounds of lean weight. Generally speaking, males should have less than 15 percent body fat and females should have less than 25 percent body fat.

Adults typically lose 5 pounds of lean (muscle) weight and gain 15 pounds of fat weight every decade of life (see figure 2.2). This appears as a 10-pound weight gain on the bathroom scale, but it really represents a 20-pound change in body components. The combined muscle loss and fat gain lead to large increases in the percentage of body fat, which is both unattractive and unhealthy. Dieting and endurance training can reduce fat weight by helping you consume fewer calories and burn off excess calories. However, neither replaces the lost muscle tissue. That's why strength training is necessary.

By combining all three—strength training, endurance exercise, and dieting—you will lose weight more easily and gain the muscle tone and cardiovascular improvements necessary for a healthy body.[4,5,6,7]

Unless you are genetically gifted, strength training is unlikely to produce a Mr. Olympia or Ms. America physique. But regular strength exercise can certainly make the difference between soft, unappealing muscles and firm, attractive muscles.

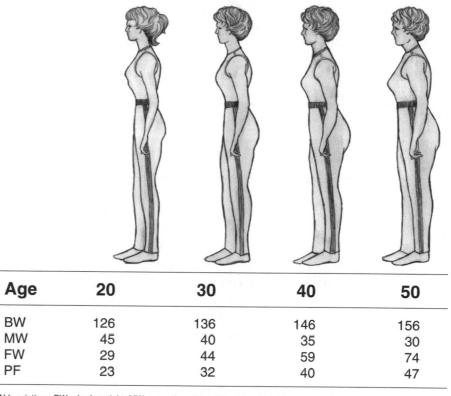

Age	20	30	40	50
BW	126	136	146	156
MW	45	40	35	30
FW	29	44	59	74
PF	23	32	40	47

Abbreviations: BW = body weight; MW = muscle weight; FW = fat weight; PF = percent fat.

■ **Figure 2.2** Body weight and body composition changes over life.

Perhaps the most common comment from new strength training participants is how much better they look as a result of their strength exercise.

3. Resting metabolism. Because muscle is very active tissue, loss of muscle as we age leads to a lower energy requirement and a reduced resting metabolic rate (the amount of energy needed to maintain the body at rest). So without strength exercise, resting metabolism decreases approximately 2 to 5 percent per decade.[8,9]

Both endurance and strength exercise increase your metabolic rate during training and for a period of time after the activity session.[10] But strength exercise also develops muscle tissue, which increases your resting metabolism 24 hours a day.

You now know that two months of strength exercise typically increases muscle mass by about three pounds. Just as impressive, three pounds of new muscle raises your resting metabolic rate by about 7 percent.[11,12] In addition, researchers at Tufts University[11] found that the strength exercisers increased their daily energy requirements by 15 percent. During the course of the study, they added three pounds of muscle, lost four pounds of fat, and increased their food intake by more than 350 calories a day. Basically, every pound of new muscle uses 30 to 40 calories a day at rest for tissue maintenance, whereas a pound of fat uses only about 2 calories a day. In other words, muscle is 15 to 20 times more metabolically active than fat.

Table 2.1 presents two women who have the same body weights but different body compositions. Note that the more fit woman has approximately five pounds more muscle tissue and uses over 200 more calories a day at rest. Because so many factors affect each person's resting metabolism, it is not possible to determine a *precise* daily calorie use for each pound of muscle tissue. However, strength training clearly increases muscle mass, and more muscle burns more calories all day long for tissue

Table 2.1 Relationship Between Muscle and Metabolism

	Body weight (lb.)	Percent fat	Fat weight	Lean weight[a]	Estimated muscle weight	Resting metabolism[b]
Tracy	100	30	30	70	35	850
Tiffany	100	20	20	80	40	1,075
Difference	—	10	10	10	5	225

[a]Data from BioAnalogics Diagnostic Medical Health Systems, Beaverton, Oregon.

[b]In calories.

maintenance. It is safe to say that more muscle definitely raises your resting metabolic rate. Imagine, you burn extra calories even while resting!

4. Physical capacity. Everything you do requires a certain percentage of your maximum strength. For example, if your maximum biceps strength is 30 pounds, carrying a 25-pound bag of dog food is a relatively difficult task that quickly becomes an all-out effort. But if you increase your maximum biceps strength to 50 pounds, carrying that same bag of dog food is a relatively easy task requiring only half of your muscular ability. Even sitting at a desk demands a degree of muscular effort, particularly from the back and neck muscles. Something has to hold up a 15-pound head all day!

Strength is also the source of power. Power is the product of muscle force and movement speed. For example, to hit a golf ball farther, you could develop more muscle force or swing the golf club faster. In a study of skilled golfers, eight weeks of strengthening and stretching exercises improved their muscle strength by almost 60 percent and increased their club head speed (golf swing) by 6 percent.[13] Progressive resistance exercise can therefore enhance athletic power by improving movement speed as well as muscle force.

5. Health enhancement. Muscle weakness is related to many degenerative diseases and increased injury potential.[8] Muscular condition affects many systems of the body and significantly affects the ability to function physically. Recent studies have identified numerous health benefits of regular strength exercise:

• Injury prevention. Weak low back muscles play a major factor in low back pain. Considering that almost 80 percent of Americans have low back problems, this is a significant finding. More important, the back patients in one study reported significantly less back discomfort after just 12 weeks of specific strength exercise for their low back muscles.[14]

Properly performed strength exercise makes muscles better shock absorbers and joint stabilizers. Training all of the major muscle groups develops a stronger musculoskeletal system and reduces the risk of muscle imbalance and overuse injuries.

• Bone mineral density. Progressive resistance exercise places stress on both the muscles and the bones. The muscles respond by increasing their fiber size, while the bones respond by increasing their protein and mineral content. Significant increases in bone density can occur after just four months of strength exercise.[15]

• Glucose metabolism. The ability to use glucose efficiently is critical for good health. In fact, poor glucose metabolism is associated with diabetes. Strength

Give It a Try . . .

Whether you are a younger adult, a middle-aged adult, or a senior, try this:

1. Measure your percent body fat.
2. Do 25 minutes of strength training and 25 minutes of endurance training (2 days per week for seniors or 3 days per week for younger and middle-aged adults) for eight weeks.
3. After eight weeks, measure your percent fat weight again.

You'll be happy with the results!

training is an effective means of improving glucose metabolism, increasing glucose uptake almost 25 percent after only four months of regular strength exercise.[16]

- Gastrointestinal transit. The time necessary to move food matter through the intestines has important health implications. Slow gastrointestinal transit time is associated with a higher risk of colon cancer. Gastrointestinal transit can be accelerated by more than 50 percent after just three months of standard strength exercise.[17]

- Cholesterol (blood lipid) levels. Although the effect of strength training on cholesterol levels needs further research, studies have demonstrated improved blood lipid profiles after several weeks of regular strength exercise.[18,19] Improvements in cholesterol levels have been similar for both endurance exercise and strength training.

- Arthritic pain. Sensible strength training may ease the discomfort of both osteoarthritis and rheumatoid arthritis.[20] In addition, by building stronger muscles, bones, and connective tissue, strength exercise enables people suffering from arthritis to function better.

- Resting blood pressure. One of the major fears among younger adults and seniors is that strength training increases blood pressure. But properly performed strength exercise is not harmful to blood pressure, even during the exercise set.[21] Strength training alone can reduce resting blood pressure in mildly hypertensive adults;[22] combining strength and endurance exercise may reduce resting blood pressure even more.[21] In a study of more than 250 adults and seniors, the participants experienced significant reductions in resting blood pressure after just eight weeks of combined strength and endurance exercise—systolic blood pressure values decreased by 5 (younger adults) and 7 (seniors), while diastolic blood pressure values decreased by 3 (younger adults) and 4 (seniors).

- Percent body fat. With epidemic levels of obesity in the United States, it is important to emphasize the role of strength training in lowering body fat percentages.[5] As indicated in figure 2.2, the average woman increases her percent body fat approximately 8 percent each decade during the midlife years. Fortunately, a large-scale study of more than 1,100 men and women between 20 and 80 years of age showed a one-point reduction in percent body fat each month of combined strength and endurance exercise.[4] In other words, a six-month training program could reduce a woman's percent body fat from an unhealthy 30 percent to a nearly ideal 24 percent.

• Depression. Many people, particularly seniors, become depressed when they can no longer do things for themselves. Loss of functionality and independence can lead to feelings of depression and anxiety. Fortunately, strength training can rebuild muscle tissue, restore muscle strength, reestablish functionality, and reduce dependence. By doing so, strength training has been shown to reverse the effects of depression and give people a new outlook on life.[23]

You can see why a sensible strength training program is beneficial for everyone!

Mechanics of Muscular Movement

A working knowledge of muscle structure and function is essential for understanding and applying the training principles for physical conditioning. That is, to most effectively work your muscles, you must know how your muscles work.

Muscle is very active tissue that makes up about half of your lean body weight. Muscle consists of approximately 75 percent water and 25 percent protein filaments (called actin and myosin). Muscle contraction occurs when the protein filaments slide together, and muscle relaxation occurs when the filaments slide apart (see figure 2.3).

Muscle fibers are the basic units of force production. They are activated by electrical impulses from the central nervous system. Regular and progressive strength exercise results in larger and stronger muscle fibers (hypertrophy), whereas lack of strength training leads to smaller, weaker muscle fibers (atrophy).

Muscle Relaxation and Contraction

Muscle relaxation is a passive process that is essential for smooth and coordinated movements. For example, when the muscle on one side of a joint (e.g., biceps) contracts and shortens, the muscle on the other side (e.g., triceps) must simultaneously relax and lengthen for productive movement to occur.

Muscle contraction initiates every movement you make. The more resistance you must overcome, the more muscle force you have to produce. An activated muscle exerts force to lift, lower, or hold a resistance. During a positive (lifting) action, the muscle produces force, shortens, and overcomes the resistance. For example, lifting a dumbbell from the hip to the shoulder requires a positive contraction of the biceps.

During a negative (lowering) action, the muscle produces force, lengthens, and is overcome by the resistance. Lowering a dumbbell from the shoulder to the hip requires a negative contraction of the biceps. During a static (holding) action, the muscle produces force but

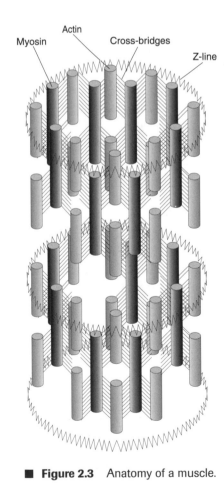

Myosin
Actin
Cross-bridges
Z-line

■ **Figure 2.3** Anatomy of a muscle.

does not change length. Holding a dumbbell at 90 degrees of elbow flexion requires a static contraction of the biceps.

Muscle Force Output

Although all three muscle actions produce force, the maximum amount of force differs because of contraction mechanics. You can actually lift about 20 percent less weight than you can hold; conversely, you can lower about 20 percent more weight than you can hold. Let's say that with maximum effort you can hold a 50-pound dumbbell at 90 degrees of elbow flexion. You will find that with maximum effort, you can lift approximately a 40-pound dumbbell from your hip to your shoulder and lower a 60-pound dumbbell from your shoulder to your hip.

As you can see, muscles are much stronger in lowering movements than in lifting movements. Therefore, from a practical training perspective, you should perform lowering movements more slowly than lifting movements to make every exercise repetition as challenging and productive as possible.

Muscle Functions

Muscles that are primarily responsible for a given joint movement are called prime mover muscles. For example, the biceps is the prime mover muscle for both the lifting and lowering phases of the dumbbell curl exercise. The muscles responsible for opposite joint movement are known as antagonist muscles. In the case of the dumbbell curl, the triceps acts as the antagonist muscle. The muscles that maintain desired body positions are referred to as stabilizer muscles. For example, when you perform dumbbell curls, the lower back muscles stabilize the torso, while the chest and upper back muscles stabilize the upper arm.

Muscle Fibers

Muscles are composed of two basic fiber types—slow-twitch and fast-twitch. Slow-twitch fibers fatigue slowly, whereas fast-twitch fibers fatigue quickly. Let's assume you have 50 muscle fibers in your biceps, of which 25 are slow-twitch and 25 are fast-twitch. You must activate 30 muscle fibers to curl a 30-pound dumbbell. Because slow-twitch fibers are recruited before fast-twitch fibers, you are able to activate 25 slow-twitch fibers and 5 fast-twitch fibers. However, since those 5 fast-twitch fibers fatigue easily, they must be replaced by 5 new fast-twitch fibers after 2 repetitions. At this rate, all 25 fast-twitch fibers will be fatigued after 10 repetitions; you will be unable to perform another dumbbell curl even though the 25 slow-twitch fibers are still functioning. Although the slow-twitch fibers perform more repetitions, the fast-twitch fibers typically experience more strength-building stimulus because they are pushed to their fatigue level. In chapter 5, strength training techniques that fatigue both kinds of fibers will be introduced for enhanced muscle development.

Motor Units

All of the muscle fibers activated by a single motor nerve are considered a motor unit. Slow-twitch motor units average about 100 slow-twitch muscle fibers, whereas fast-twitch motor units average about 500 fast-twitch muscle fibers. Lifting a light dumbbell (e.g., 10 pounds) requires few motor units (slow-twitch); therefore, many repetitions are possible. However, lifting a 50-pound dumbbell requires many motor units (both slow- and fast-twitch), so few repetitions are possible. During the early stages of strength training, much of the performance improvement is due to better motor unit selection, referred to as motor learning.

Muscle Fatigue and Soreness

Although many physiological factors may contribute to momentary muscle fatigue, lactic acid accumulation undoubtedly plays a major role. Lactic acid is released during anaerobic energy production, and fatigue sets in as it builds up in the blood and muscles. Excess lactic acid increases tissue acidity, which apparently activates pain sensors and prevents further muscle contraction. Fortunately, momentary muscle fatigue passes quickly and should not be a deterrent to strength training exercise.

High-effort strength workouts may produce muscle discomfort a day or two after the training session. This delayed-onset muscle soreness is associated with negative muscle actions and most likely results from microscopic tears within the muscle fibers. You should train in a manner that avoids heavy tissue microtrauma, which may require several recovery days for the repair process to be completed.

Limb Length

Strength performance depends a lot on the lever systems formed by your muscles, tendons, and bones. Other things being equal, people with shorter levers (arms and legs) have a strength advantage over people with longer levers. The following formula is used to determine how much resistance your biceps can hold at a right angle:

$$resistance = (muscle\ force \times muscle\ lever)\ /\ resistance\ lever$$

Let's assume that your biceps produces 300 pounds of force and that you have a 1-inch muscle lever (distance from your elbow joint to your muscle insertion point). If you have a 10-inch resistance lever (forearm), you can hold a 30-pound dumbbell at a right angle (see figure 2.4). If you have a 12-inch resistance lever (forearm), you can hold only a 25-pound dumbbell at a right angle. Although the muscle force and muscle insertion points are the same, the shorter forearm provides a distinct strength advantage.

Muscle Insertion Point

Another leverage factor that has a major influence on strength performance is the muscle insertion point. This is the distance between the joint and the muscle attachment that functions as the muscle lever. Generally, people who have muscle insertion points that are farther from the joint have a strength advantage over persons with closer muscle insertion points. Once again, the formula for determining how much resistance your biceps can hold at a right angle is

$$resistance = (muscle\ force \times muscle\ lever)\ /\ resistance\ lever.$$

Let's assume that your biceps produces 300 pounds of force and that your forearm forms a 10-inch resistance lever. If you have a 1.2-inch muscle lever (distance from your elbow joint to your muscle insertion point), you can hold a 36-pound dumbbell at a right angle (see figure 2.5). If you have a 1-inch muscle lever, you can hold only a 30-pound dumbbell at a right angle. Although the muscle force and forearm length are the same, the farther muscle insertion point provides a definite strength advantage.

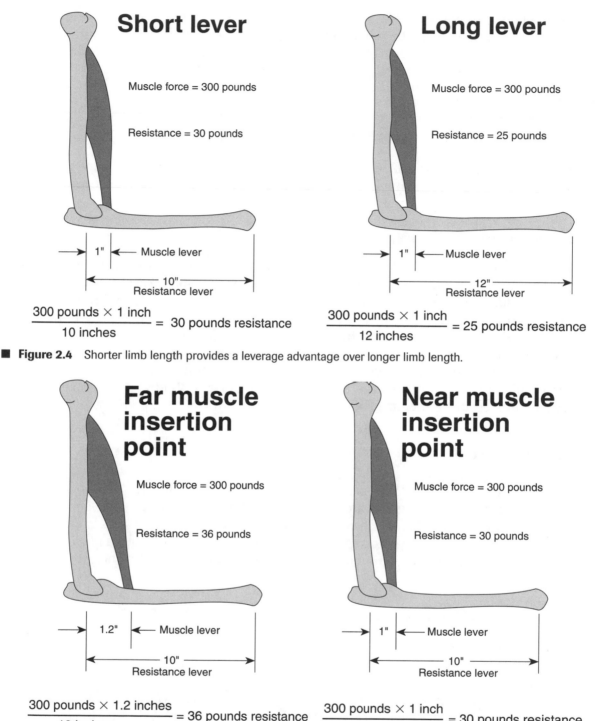

Figure 2.4 Shorter limb length provides a leverage advantage over longer limb length.

Figure 2.5 Farther muscle insertion point provides a leverage advantage over closer muscle insertion point.

Muscle Length

When you compare the length of a muscle with its connecting tendon, you will find that different people have different ratios of muscle length to tendon length. Most people have medium-length muscles with medium-length tendons, while some people have relatively short muscles with long tendons, and others have relatively long muscles with short tendons.

People who have relatively short muscles have a lower potential for building large muscle size, whereas those with relatively long muscles have a higher potential for building large muscle size. Although everyone has the capacity to build larger muscles, most successful bodybuilders have the genetic advantage of relatively long muscles throughout their bodies.

Types of Exercise

You can exercise your muscles differently depending on the type of resistance you use in your training program. Effectiveness, safety, and personal preference are key factors when selecting your exercise mode.

Isometric Exercise

Isometric exercise involves static muscle contraction done against a stationary resistance, such as pushing against the top of a doorway. Isometric exercise effectively builds muscle strength, but its lack of movement is associated with certain training problems. First, isometric exercise increases muscle strength only at the joint positions used. To develop full-range muscle strength with isometrics, it is necessary to train at several positions throughout the movement range.

Second, static muscle contractions tend to block blood flow, which may produce unsafe blood pressure responses. For this reason, older individuals and persons with cardiovascular problems should avoid isometric forms of exercise.

Give It a Try . . .

To estimate the relative length of your biceps, make a hard biceps contraction with your elbow at a right angle and your wrist turned inward. Now, place as many fingers as possible between your forearm and the end of the bulge your biceps makes. If you can place three fingers in the gap, you have a relatively short biceps. If you can place two fingers in the gap, you have a medium-length biceps, and if you can place only one finger in the gap, you have a relatively long biceps (see figure 2.6).

Long—one finger's width   Medium—two fingers' width   Short—three fingers' width

■ **Figure 2.6**   Estimating biceps length.

Third, most people have difficulty assessing their exercise effort and training progress with isometric strengthening programs. The lack of movement makes monotony and motivation serious obstacles to regular isometric training.

Isokinetic Exercise

Although there are a few exceptions, isokinetic exercise generally involves only positive muscle contractions against an accommodating hydraulic or electronic resistance. The training device maintains a constant movement speed, and the muscle force you apply determines the resistance force you receive. That is, if you apply low muscle force, you receive low resistance force, and if you apply high muscle force, you receive high resistance force. For example, if you use a low-effort arm stroke when swimming, you encounter low resistance from the water, but if you use a high-effort arm stroke, you encounter high resistance from the water. Therefore, isokinetic resistance is somewhat "soft." If you inadvertently exert less muscle effort, you automatically encounter less resistance and so gain fewer benefits.

Isotonic Exercise

Isotonic exercise has several differences in comparison with isokinetic exercise. First, isotonic exercise includes both positive and negative muscle contractions. Second, isotonic exercise does not require a constant movement speed. For example, you may lift the barbell in two seconds and lower the barbell in four seconds. Third, you control your effort level by selecting a certain resistance force and your muscles must respond accordingly. In other words, the more resistance you select, the more muscle force you must exert to perform each repetition.

Isotonic exercise, the most popular and effective type of strength training, may be performed with a constant resistance or with a variable resistance. Although the same principles apply, each type of resistance has a different pattern of muscle force production.

Dynamic Constant Resistance Exercise

Dynamic constant resistance exercise uses a fixed resistance such as a barbell. Although the resistance does not change, leverage factors cause your muscle force to be lower in some positions and higher in other positions. In figure 2.7, the barbell provides 100 pounds of resistance force throughout the pressing movement, even though movement mechanics permit the muscle force to increase from 100 pounds in the bottom position to 140 pounds in the top position. Consequently, this form of isotonic exercise may provide a poor matching of muscle force and resistance force throughout the movement range.

Dynamic Variable Resistance Exercise

As the name implies, dynamic variable resistance exercise uses a resistance that changes throughout the movement range. For example, Nautilus machines incorporate a cam to automatically vary the resistance, matching your muscle force pattern. That is, you encounter proportionately less resistance in positions of lower muscle force and proportionately more resistance in positions of higher muscle force. The Nautilus machine smoothly increases the resistance from 100 pounds in the bottom position to 140 pounds in the top position (see figure 2.8). This results in a better matching of muscle force and resistance force throughout the movement range,

■ **Figure 2.7** Dynamic constant resistance exercise may provide a poor matching of muscle force and resistance force.

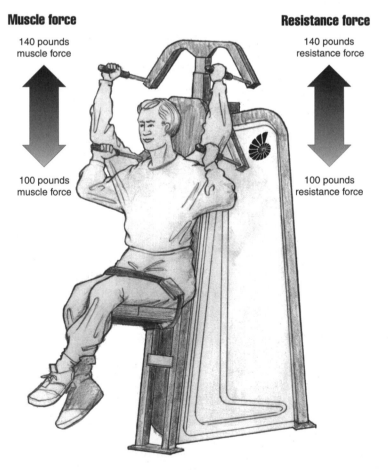

■ **Figure 2.8** Dynamic variable resistance exercise provides a good matching of muscle force and resistance force because of the cam, which automatically changes resistance force.

which makes this form of isotonic exercise a more productive means of strength training. Consequently, training on a well-designed variable resistance machine may be more effective and efficient than standard free weight training.

Now that you know how your muscles work, you'll want to know how to work your muscles safely and productively. Although there are many different training programs for increasing muscle strength, some pose a high risk of injury, while others require a major time commitment. What you need is a program that has been thoroughly tested for safe, effective, and efficient strength development.

Basic Strength Training Guidelines

Although relatively simple in concept, the following procedures are so productive that many military bases, police academies, and professional football teams follow them.

A sound strength training program should include exercises for all of the major muscle groups. If you select your exercises carefully, your muscles will develop in balance with each other and you'll have a firm foundation for further improvement. Do not emphasize some muscle groups over others because this can result in muscle imbalance injuries. For example, when I was a university track coach, I had my sprinters perform strengthening exercises for their quadriceps muscles and stretching exercises for their hamstring muscles. Unfortunately, this procedure produced relatively strong quadriceps and relatively weak hamstrings, which set the stage for hamstring strains. I soon learned the importance of a comprehensive training program to develop overall muscle strength and to reduce the risk of injury.

Do your best to exercise larger muscle groups first, followed by medium and smaller muscle groups. For example, you may begin with the legs, then work the torso, arms, midsection, and neck. You should also try to pair exercises, working opposing muscle groups in succession.

Table 2.2 shows the machine and free weight exercises that best address the major and minor muscles in general order of larger to smaller groups, with opposing muscle groups paired for muscle balance.

Frequency

Properly performed strength exercise progressively stresses your muscles and produces some degree of tissue microtrauma. After your training session, the stressed tissue undergoes repair and building processes that lead to larger and stronger muscles. Muscles usually need between 48 and 72 hours to complete these physiological changes, and each new workout should take place at the peak of this muscle-building process. Unfortunately, the only way to determine your most productive recovery and building period is through trial and error. That's why it is so important to maintain a detailed record of each training session. If your exercise frequency is appropriate, you should notice some strength improvements every workout.

Generally speaking, two or three strength training sessions a week provide excellent results for most people.[24] Ideally, you should aim for three strength training sessions a week. However, if that's just too much for your schedule, remember that two strength workouts a week may produce 75 to 85 percent as much muscle improvement as three strength workouts a week. Two days are better than none, so don't let time pressures prevent you from training.

Perhaps as important as exercise frequency is training consistency. Try to stay on your training schedule and avoid back-to-back strength workouts. For example, it's

Table 2.2 Nautilus and Free Weight Exercises That Best Address the Major Muscle Groups

Major muscle groups	Nautilus machines	Free weights
Quadriceps	Leg extension, leg press	Squat, lunge, step-up, deadlift
Hamstrings	Seated leg curl, prone leg curl, leg press	Squat, lunge, step-up, deadlift
Hip adductors	Hip adduction	
Hip abductors	Hip abduction	
Pectoralis major	Chest cross, pec dec, 10° chest, bench press, incline press, vertical chest, assisted bar dip	Bench fly, incline fly, bench press, incline press, bar dip
Latissimus dorsi	Pullover, compound row, pulldown, assisted chin-up	Pullover, pulldown, bent row, chin-up
Deltoids	Lateral raise, overhead press	Lateral raise, shoulder press
Biceps	Preacher curl, biceps curl	Preacher curl, barbell curl
Triceps	Low triceps extension, high triceps extension	Overhead triceps extension, triceps pressdown, triceps kickback
Erector spinae	Low back	Trunk extension
Rectus abdominis	Abdominal, knee lift	Trunk curl
Obliques	Rotary torso	Twisting knee-lift trunk curl
Neck	4-way neck	Shoulder shrug
Calves	Seated calf	Heel raise

not a good idea to train too sporadically, and it is usually counterproductive to work the same muscles two days in a row.

Sets

In 1990, the American College of Sports Medicine (ACSM) recommended one or more sets of each resistance exercise for strength development.[25] While it is obvious that you must perform at least one set of strength work, most people are unaware that additional sets may have little extra value. Research in both upper body and lower body strength training has shown that doing single-sets versus multiple-sets over a 10- and 14-week training period achieved similar results.[26,27,28] So why do more than necessary to get to the same place?

Exercise Resistance

For decades, the overload principle has been the key concept in strength training. Overloading involves using progressively heavier resistance to work the muscles harder, encouraging further strength development. For example, if you can curl 100 pounds one time, then one repetition with 105 pounds will overload your biceps. Or if you can curl 50 pounds 20 times, then 20 repetitions with 55 pounds would also overload your biceps.

Using a relatively high resistance increases the chances of injury, while doing a relatively high number of repetitions decreases strength benefits. So what are the best guidelines for applying the overload principle? Muscle strength can be best developed by working the target muscle to fatigue within the anaerobic energy system. This is the system that supplies energy for high-effort exercise lasting less than 90 seconds. For most practical purposes, about 50 to 70 seconds of continuous muscle work to the point of muscle fatigue is preferred. Most people can perform about 50 to 70 seconds of resistance exercise with 75 percent of their maximum weight load (75 percent of the heaviest weight they can lift one time). At a moderate speed (about 6 seconds a repetition), this corresponds to 8 to 12 controlled repetitions.

Fortunately, you can estimate 75 percent of your maximum resistance without doing an all-out lift. Simply find the weight that you can lift 10 times to fatigue and this should be about 75 percent of your maximum. Training at this weight level creates a high strength stimulus and poses a low risk of injury. Although 75 percent of maximum resistance is standard strength training procedure, periodically training with lower and higher percentages of your maximum resistance offers you a welcome change of pace, giving you both physiological and psychological benefits.

Repetitions

An inverse relationship exists between the amount of resistance you use and the number of repetitions you can perform. That is, you can complete fewer repetitions with a relatively heavy resistance and more repetitions with a relatively light resistance.

Another less obvious factor influences the number of repetitions you can manage with a given resistance. If you have inherited predominantly fast-twitch muscle fibers, you will have lower muscle endurance and perform fewer repetitions than average with a specific resistance. If you have inherited predominantly slow-twitch muscle fibers, you will have higher muscle endurance and perform more repetitions than average with a specific resistance.

To learn more about repetitions, we assessed almost 150 exercisers who had been using the same training procedures.[29] Most of the subjects completed between 8 and 12 repetitions in 50 to 70 seconds with 75 percent of their maximum resistance. They were average individuals who had moderate muscle endurance (even mix of fast-twitch and slow-twitch muscle fibers). A small number of subjects performed 5 to 8 repetitions in 30 to 50 seconds. These were power athletes (sprinters) who had low muscle endurance (i.e., high percentage of fast-twitch muscle fibers). At the other extreme, a few participants performed 12 to 16 repetitions in 70 to 90 seconds. These were endurance athletes (distance runners) who had high muscle endurance (i.e., high percentage of slow-twitch muscle fibers).

Based on these findings and follow-up research that matched the exercise duration to each individual's muscle endurance, the following repetition guidelines are recommended. People with low-endurance muscles generally attain better results by training with about 5 to 8 repetitions (30 to 50 seconds) a set. People with moderate-endurance muscles generally achieve better results by training with about 8 to 12 repetitions (50 to 70 seconds) a set. People with high-endurance muscles generally gain better results by training with about 12 to 15 repetitions (70 to 90 seconds) a set. Because most people have moderate-endurance muscles, 8 to 12 repetitions a set are suggested as standard training procedure. Still, you may periodically perform greater or fewer repetitions a set for a change of pace.

Progression

Continued strength development depends on progressive resistance exercise that gradually places more stress on the target muscles. A double-progressive training system in which you alternately add repetitions and resistance is generally preferred. For example, maybe you can do eight lateral raises with 50 pounds. Continue training with 50 pounds until you can do 12 repetitions, then increase the resistance by about 5 percent. That is, add 2.5 pounds to the weight stack and train with 52.5 pounds until you can again do 12 repetitions.

By systematically increasing the exercise repetitions up to 12 and then increasing the exercise resistance by 5 percent (or less), you ensure gradual strength gains with the lowest risk of injury. Although there are other progression protocols, this system fatigues the target muscles with 50 to 70 seconds of continuous resistance exercise and almost eliminates the possibility of doing too much too soon.

Speed

Exercise speed may be divided into three categories: fast, moderate, and slow. A fast exercise speed is one that you cannot stop at a given point in the movement range. Fast exercise speed emphasizes momentum, which reduces muscle effort but increases the risk of injury. Lifting movements under two seconds qualify as fast. A moderate exercise speed is one that you can stop. Moderate exercise speed de-emphasizes momentum, increasing muscle effort and reducing the risk of injury. Lifting movements between two and four seconds are of moderate speed. A slow exercise speed is one that you completely control. Slow exercise speed minimizes momentum and maximizes muscle tension. Lifting movements over four seconds are considered slow. Research indicates that moderate to slow exercise speeds are effective for increasing muscle strength, and they are recommended for safe and successful strength training.[30]

Moderate to slow exercise speeds have the following training advantages over fast exercise speeds:

- A longer period of muscle tension
- A higher level of muscle force
- A lower level of momentum
- A lower risk of tissue injury

Six-second repetitions, with two seconds for the lifting movements and four seconds for the lowering movements, have a long history of success. The longer lowering phase places more emphasis on the negative muscle contraction. Although six-second repetitions may be considered standard training procedure, using other moderate-to-slow movement speeds is certainly acceptable.

Range

You should perform full-range movements to develop full-range muscle strength. This is necessary because muscle strength is somewhat specific to the movement range that is trained. For example, back extensions performed in one-half of the movement range have their greatest strengthening effect in that area.[31]

Full-range muscle strength is especially important for patients with low back pain. People who have little strength in the position of full trunk extension may be more likely to experience low back pain. Fortunately, strength training the lower back muscles through their full movement range can significantly reduce pain in this part of the body.[32]

Because full-range muscle strength enhances physical performance and reduces the risk of injury, you should perform full-range resistance exercise whenever possible. Although the range of joint movement varies among individuals, you should train from the position of full muscle stretch to the position of complete muscle contraction. Keep in mind that when the target muscle (e.g., biceps) is fully contracted, the opposing muscle (e.g., triceps) is fully stretched. For this reason, full-range resistance training may enhance joint flexibility as well as increase muscle strength.[3]

Designing Your Program

You know by now that strength exercises improve muscular fitness and endurance exercises improve cardiovascular fitness. Begin your workout with whichever type of exercise you want; you can achieve similar strength gains regardless of the activity order.

Perform the activity that is most important to you first. For example, if your primary goal is muscular fitness, do the strength exercise first. If your main objective is cardiovascular fitness, do the endurance exercise first. Whichever activity order you prefer, begin each training session with a few minutes of warm-up exercise and end with a few minutes of cool-down exercise. These transition phases between rest and vigorous physical activity may provide important physiological and psychological benefits. Easy walking and cycling are appropriate activities for warming up and cooling down.

Strength and Stretching

You should perform strength exercises to improve muscular fitness and stretching exercises to improve joint flexibility. However, we have found that doing both activities within the same training session can actually enhance your strength gains.[33,34] The ability of muscle tissue to contract and shorten as well as to relax and lengthen represents two sides of the same coin. Performing both activities in the same workout enhances the muscle's response to the strength exercise.

Breathing

Don't forget to breathe! Breathe continuously while performing strength exercise. Regardless of the exercise effort, you should never hold your breath. The internal pressure caused by holding your breath coupled with the external pressure of forceful muscle contractions may limit blood flow to the brain and heart. To avoid light-headedness and high blood pressure, breathe continuously throughout every exercise set. Exhale during lifting movements and inhale during lowering movements. This decreases the internal air pressure as the external muscular pressure increases and vice versa.

Intensity

High-intensity exercise enhances strength development.[36] Your exercise effort should be hard enough to fatigue the target muscles within the anaerobic energy system

Real-Life Results . . .

During the past several years, we have completed numerous research studies with average adults, seniors, children, and several special populations. All of the studies showed significant improvements in muscle strength and body composition, as well as in selected variables such as joint flexibility, balance control, power production, athletic performance, posture, and self-confidence. Two studies in particular demonstrated the strength training achievements of the participants.

Study A[4]

Subjects: 1,132 men and women in age brackets 21 to 40, 41 to 60, and 61 to 80

Duration: Eight weeks of basic strength and endurance training

Regimen: One set of 8 to 12 repetitions of 12 standard exercises, two or three days a week, as well as 20 minutes of walking or cycling

Results: Adult exercisers added about 2.5 pounds of muscle, lost approximately 4.5 pounds of fat, and reduced their resting blood pressure by almost four points. They also increased their overall muscle strength by more than 40 percent. The men gained muscle and lost fat at a faster rate than the women, but the younger (21 to 40 years), middle-aged (41 to 60 years), and older (61 to 80 years) adults experienced similar improvements in body composition. The simplicity of the basic training program was well received by the participants, and more than 90 percent continued to do their strength workouts after completing the eight-week exercise study.

Study B[35]

Subjects: Frail elderly patients at an assisted-care senior living center, mostly confined to wheelchairs, with an average age of 89 years

Duration: 14 weeks of brief strength training

Regimen: Six resistance exercises (leg press, triceps press, seated row, low back extension, neck extension, and neck flexion); one set of 8 to 12 repetitions, two days a week

Results: Elderly participants added about four pounds of muscle, lost almost three pounds of fat, increased their leg strength by more than 80 percent, increased their upper body strength by almost 40 percent, enhanced their joint flexibility by approximately 30 percent, and improved their functional independence measure by 14 percent. For example, almost all of the patients spent less time in their wheelchairs, one patient no longer used a wheelchair, and one patient left the assisted-living residence to rejoin her husband in an independent-living apartment. Even with frail elderly individuals, the basic strength training procedures produce impressive and important improvements in body composition, musculoskeletal function, and quality of life.

(about 50 to 70 seconds). This typically requires 8 to 12 repetitions with 75 percent of your maximum resistance. For best results, use moderate to slow exercise speed, full-range movement, and correct performance technique.

Summary

Sensible strength training provides many health and fitness benefits related to muscle development. Understanding how muscles work and designing a program that fits your goals and schedule will help you start (and continue) a strength training program that is right for you!

Strength Training Equipment

Some people don't like technology. They prefer the simplicity of doing strength exercise without the bother of equipment, whether it's fancy or simple. They do sit-ups for their midsections, push-ups for their upper bodies, and knee bends for their lower bodies. But although these body weight exercises are beneficial up to a point, they don't permit progressive increases in training resistance. To better develop muscle strength, you must use enough resistance to fatigue the target muscles within the anaerobic energy system (typically 8 to 12 repetitions in 50 to 70 seconds). As you become stronger and perform more repetitions, you must add resistance to maintain a desirable repetition range.

Development of Strength Training Equipment

Because body weight exercises limit you to a single resistance, strength building enthusiasts have developed exercise equipment with adjustable weight loads.

Early Strength Training Equipment

The basic barbell, introduced around the turn of the 20th century, was one of the first adjustable strength training tools. As you gain strength, added barbell plates increase the weight load. Barbell training offers a simple, effective, and versatile form of resistance exercise. However, some barbell exercises require spotters for safe performance (e.g., squats, bench presses). Dumbbell training eliminates this safety concern and offers even more exercise versatility. Of course, both barbell and dumbbell training require gripping the bars firmly, which involves the forearm muscles in every free weight exercise. When handled in a careful and controlled manner, free weights provide balanced and comprehensive strength training exercise with attention to stabilizer muscles as well as prime mover groups.

Resistance Exercise Machines

The next step in strength training equipment was the introduction of weight-stack machines. The weight stacks, which always travel vertically against gravity, are moved by means of attached handles or cables. These machines offer the convenience of changing resistance by merely inserting a pin and the safety feature of never being trapped under a heavy barbell.

In 1970, Arthur Jones developed a new line of Nautilus resistance machines that attempt to imitate the muscle–joint function of the body. For example, the super pullover machine for the upper back (latissimus dorsi) muscles incorporates several unique design features (see figure 3.1). The first functional design feature is a *rotary movement* arm that revolves around the shoulder joint axis to better isolate the latissimus dorsi muscle and match human movement mechanics.

The second functional design feature is *direct resistance* with movement pads that contact the upper arms. The resistance force is applied directly to the upper arm where the latissimus dorsi muscle attaches. Placing the resistance force against the upper arm rather than against the hand eliminates using the smaller forearm and biceps muscles, which usually tire before the larger latissimus dorsi.

The third functional design feature is *variable resistance,* accomplished by an oval-shaped cam that automatically changes the resistance force throughout the exercise movement. The cam proportionately increases the resistance in stronger segments of the movement range and proportionately decreases the resistance in weaker segments of the movement range. In this way, variable resistance tries to keep resistance force and muscle force well matched throughout the movement. This virtually eliminates sticking points, or places in the movement range where the resistance is too heavy.

Movement and Resistance

The Nautilus design features—rotary movement, direct resistance, and variable resistance—made the super pullover a safe, effective, and efficient machine for strengthening the latissimus dorsi muscle. Jones later developed similar machines that targeted the other major muscle groups, concentrating on nine strength training factors known collectively as *full-range exercise.* Full-range exercise means that each training repetition is as productive as possible for stimulating strength development. This is accomplished through positive work,

■ **Figure 3.1** Super pullover machine.

Free Weights Versus Resistance Machines

Free weights

- Inexpensive
- Provide resistance for most major muscle groups
- Portable and easy to store
- Indestructible

Resistance machines

- Isolate target muscle and match resistance force to potential muscle force
- Maintain stable movement to enhance performance and reduce risk of injury
- Change resistance by moving a pin within the weight plates
- Provide specific path movement to keep joint action on track throughout each set
- Provide full-range movement

negative work, rotary movement, direct resistance, variable resistance, balanced resistance, resistance in full contraction, resistance in full stretch, and unrestricted movement speed. Table 3.1 shows how various types of resistance equipment address these nine factors of full-range strength training, which are discussed in the following paragraphs.

- Positive work. Positive work refers to resistance during positive (concentric) muscle contractions, which is the lifting phase of the exercise. Strength training that uses static (isometric) muscle contractions runs a high risk of cardiovascular problems due to increased blood pressure. Strength training that uses only negative (eccentric) muscle contractions with heavier than normal resistance runs a high risk of muscular injury. Full-range exercise begins with positive work (see figure 3.2).

Table 3.1   Various Types of Resistance Equipment and Full-Range Exercise

	Typical isokinetic equipment	Free weights	Typical weight-stack machine
Positive work	All exercises	All exercises	All exercises
Negative work	No exercises	All exercises	All exercises
Rotary movement	All major muscle groups	Most major muscle groups	Most major muscle groups
Direct resistance	All major muscle groups	Some major muscle groups	Most major muscle groups
Variable resistance	All exercises	No exercises	Some exercises
Balanced resistance	No exercises	All exercises	Some exercises
Resistance in full contraction	No exercises	Most exercises	All exercises
Resistance in full stretch	No exercises	Most exercises	Most exercises
Unrestricted movement speed	No exercises	Most exercises	All exercises

• Negative work. Negative work refers to resistance during negative (eccentric) muscle contractions, which is the lowering phase of the exercise. Because eccentric contractions cause more tissue microtrauma, negative work increases the strength-building stimulus. Remember that the same muscle lifts (positive contraction) and lowers (negative contraction) the resistance. Like positive work, negative work is an essential component of full-range exercise (see figure 3.3).

• Rotary movement. Every muscle contracts in a linear (straight line) movement. But the bone attached to the contracting muscle is pulled in a rotary (curved) movement. Consequently, to isolate a muscle, you must do rotary exercises (see figure 3.4). For example, the leg extension is a rotary exercise that isolates the quadriceps muscles; the leg curl is a rotary exercise that isolates the hamstring muscles. In contrast, the leg press is a linear exercise that involves both the quadriceps and hamstrings. It is an excellent strength-building exercise that should be included in your overall training program, but it does not isolate a specific muscle group. Full-range training should include rotary movements that target each major muscle group.

• Direct resistance. To isolate a muscle most effectively, the resistance must be applied directly to the body part attached to that muscle. For example, to best isolate the deltoids, the resistance should be applied to the upper arms where the deltoids attach. This is why the lateral raise machine places the resistance pads directly against the upper arms (see figure 3.5). In contrast, the shoulder press applies the resistance to the hands, involving muscles in the forearms and upper arms as well as the deltoids. In conjunction with rotary movement, direct resistance enables you to effectively isolate the target muscle, an important component of full-range exercise.

• Variable resistance. Because of leverage factors, your muscle force is higher in some positions and lower in others. As a result, constant resistance exercise gives enough resistance in some parts of the movement range but not enough resistance in other parts of the movement range. For example, during a leg press exercise you can apply 2.5 times more force in the last part than in the first part of the movement. Consequently, a well-designed leg press machine provides about 2.5 times as much

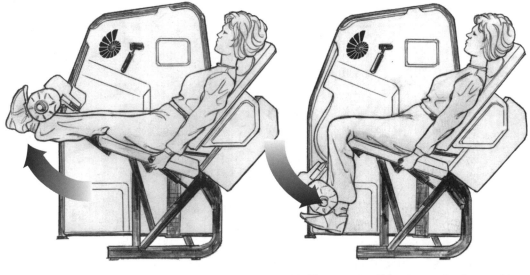

■ **Figure 3.2** Positive-work phase of leg extension exercise.

■ **Figure 3.3** Negative-work phase of leg extension exercise.

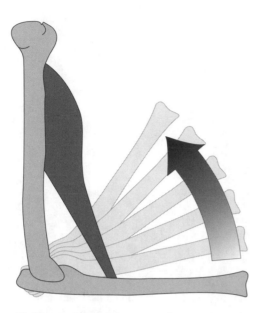

■ **Figure 3.4** Every muscle contracts in a straight line, which pulls the attached bone in a rotary movement.

■ **Figure 3.5** Direct resistance applies resistance force directly to the target muscle.

resistance in the end range of motion. One means of effectively and proportionately varying the resistance force is an oval-shaped cam apparatus (see figure 3.6).

• Balanced resistance. All exercise machines have moving parts that add and subtract resistance force depending on the position of the movement arms. Well-designed machines are constructed with counterbalances to eliminate undesirable variations in the resistance force (see figure 3.7). The counterbalances cancel out the weight of the movement arms so that the only resistance changes are those produced by the cam. Balanced resistance helps deliver the necessary resistance force throughout your exercise movement.

• Resistance in full contraction. When you move a barbell outside the vertical plane, as some free weight exercises require, there may be no opposing resistance when the muscles are fully contracted. For example, when you perform dumbbell preacher bench curls, the muscular effort drops off once the arms cross the vertical plane. At this point in the movement, gravity works for you, rather than against you, so there is no effective resistance when the biceps is fully contracted. Machines that incorporate vertical weight stacks eliminate this problem because the resistance always moves directly against the force of gravity.

• Resistance in full stretch. Full-range exercise requires that the target muscles work against appropriate resistance in every part of the movement range, including the position of full muscle stretch. Because of the interference of the bar itself, some barbell exercises do not allow resistance in the fully stretched position. The standing curl and bench press are examples of this problem. Well-designed machines have movement arms that provide variable resistance throughout the normal range of joint action, including the position of full muscle stretch.

• Unrestricted movement speed. As presented in chapter 2, isometric exercise has no movement, whereas isokinetic exercise has a fixed movement speed. Weight-stack machines provide a form of isotonic exercise that features both variable resistance and variable movement speed. Although fast training speeds are not advised because of inertia and momentum, no set speed for performing strength

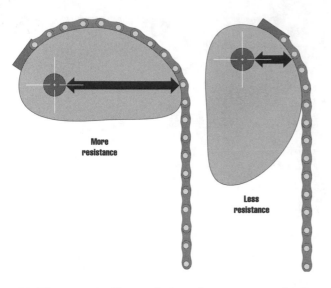

■ **Figure 3.6** The oval-shaped cam automatically changes the resistance force by moving the chain closer to, or farther from, the axis of rotation.

■ **Figure 3.7** Machine movement arms with counter-balances are designed to provide appropriate resistance throughout the exercise movement.

exercise exists. In fact, as mentioned earlier, standard strength training involves two different movement speeds for every repetition. You should lift the weight load in about two seconds and lower it in about four seconds. By using these two movement speeds, you challenge the target muscles during both the weaker positive contraction (lifting phase) and the stronger negative contraction (lowering phase).

Summary

Free weights provide a simple and effective means of doing progressive resistance exercise. You can use barbells and dumbbells for a variety of exercises. They take up little space and are almost maintenance-free, but they require careful instruction and safety awareness. However, exercise machines were designed to offer full-range strength training, including nine specific exercise components, such as rotary movement, direct resistance, and variable resistance, while offering a full range of positive and negative work, balanced resistance, and unrestricted movement speed. Whichever equipment you choose to employ in your strength training program, remember to follow the recommended guidelines and perform exercises accurately to ensure maximum results with no injury.

Strength Training Exercises

Now you're ready to learn specific strength training exercises. Your job is to perform each exercise properly to enhance your rate of strength development. The exercises are grouped under the following seven categories based on the major muscles addressed:

1. Leg exercises
2. Chest exercises
3. Upper back exercises
4. Shoulder exercises
5. Arm exercises
6. Midsection exercises
7. Neck exercises

In the following chapters, you will learn which exercises to do first and how to design specific exercise programs as you progress. Photographs of the beginning and ending positions accompany each exercise description. Nautilus equipment is featured for the machine exercises because it is uniquely designed to provide all nine factors of full-range strength training, as discussed in chapter 3. Both barbells and dumbbells are featured for the free weight exercises, depending on performance and safety considerations.

Before You Begin

Before you begin working out, determine how each exercise fits into your overall training program. You must also be comfortable with the equipment and confident in your exercise technique. To gain a complete overview, be sure to read through both this chapter and the next before establishing your strength training routine.

Pre-Performance Checkpoints

Before starting the exercise set, check these key factors related to positioning and performance:

Machines

Follow these safety guidelines before you begin any machine exercise:

1. Make sure you have placed the desired resistance on the weight stack. Check both weight-stack selector pins for proper insertion.

2. Double-check the seat position to make sure that the joint axis of rotation is in line with the machine axis of rotation (rotary exercises) or set for a full range of joint movement (linear exercises). When you are properly positioned, the cam will correctly change the resistance to match the target muscle's strength throughout the exercise movement.

3. If a seat belt is provided, be sure to fasten it snugly around your waist (e.g., super pullover machine) or legs (e.g., low back machine). Seat belts serve as anchors that help maintain proper body alignment as you exercise.

4. Sit with proper posture and good back support. Your head should be in a neutral (upright) position on most machines.

Free Weights

Follow these guidelines before you begin any free weight exercise:

1. Make sure floor space in the exercise area is uncluttered.

2. Place precisely the correct combination of weight plates on the barbell or dumbbells.

3. Fasten all plate collars securely, and double check before each exercise set.

4. Test bench stability and support rack security before each use.

5. Examine cables, handles, and attachments for excessive wear and weakness.

Exercise Performance

When you perform strength exercises, observe the following points to maximize muscle development and minimize injury risk:

• Perform each exercise slowly, about two seconds for lifting and four seconds for lowering. This standard six-second training procedure has consistently produced excellent results. The lowering phase is slower than the lifting phase to make the stronger negative muscle contractions more challenging.

• Perform each exercise through a full movement range. This is necessary for comprehensive muscle conditioning from the fully stretched to the fully contracted positions.

• Perform one or more sets of each exercise. Single-set training is an effective and efficient means of increasing muscle strength and size.

• Use a weight load that fatigues the target muscles within 8 to 12 repetitions to emphasize the anaerobic energy system (about 50 to 70 seconds) and to optimize strength development.

• Increase the weight load by 5 percent when 12 repetitions can be completed. Gradual training progression is the key to continued strength improvement with minimum risk of injuries.

• Breathe continuously throughout every repetition, exhaling while lifting and inhaling while lowering. This breathing pattern should reduce the chance of an excessive blood pressure response while enhancing exercise performance.

• Never compromise proper form for additional repetitions. Use proper technique to make sure that you are training the target muscles productively and safely.

The rest of the chapter outlines various strength training exercises and the proper way to perform them. Exercises for the larger muscle groups will be described first, followed by exercises for the smaller muscle groups. This way, you will work with heavier weight loads when you are fresh and lighter weight loads when you are fatigued. This does not mean that the smaller muscles are less important than the larger muscles. Rather, it is physiologically and psychologically better to perform higher-energy exercises (e.g., leg presses) before lower-energy exercises (e.g., triceps extensions).

LEG EXTENSION

Joint action

Knee extension

Prime mover muscles

Quadriceps

Movement path

Rotary

Exercise technique

Sit on seat and place legs behind adjustable movement pad. Align knees with machine axis of rotation. Push seat-adjust lever to bring seat back against hips. Grip handles lightly. Lift movement pad until quadriceps are fully contracted. Return slowly to starting position and repeat.

Technique tips

■ Keep back against seat.

■ Maintain neutral head position.

■ Keep ankles in neutral position (about 90 degrees).

■ Exhale throughout extending action.

LEG EXTENSION

A

B

SEATED LEG CURL

Joint action

Knee flexion

Prime mover muscles

Hamstrings

Movement path

Rotary

Exercise technique

Sit on seat, push leg entry handle forward, slide legs between adjustable movement pads, and return handle to resting position. Align knees with machine axis of rotation. Push seat-adjust lever to bring seat back against hips. Grip handles lightly. Curl movement pad toward hips until hamstrings are fully contracted. Return slowly to starting position and repeat.

Technique tips

- Keep back against seat.
- Maintain neutral head position.
- Keep ankles in flexed position (toes pointed toward shins).
- Exhale throughout curling action.

SEATED LEG CURL

A

B

37

PRONE LEG CURL

Joint action

Knee flexion

Prime mover muscles

Hamstrings

Movement path

Rotary

Exercise technique

Stand between bench seat and adjustable movement pad. Lie face down with legs straight and knees just off bench in line with machine axis of rotation. Grip handles lightly. Pull movement pads to hips by contracting hamstrings. Return slowly to starting position and repeat.

Technique tips

- Keep chin on bench seat.
- Maintain hip support throughout exercise movement.
- Keep ankles in flexed position (toes toward shins).
- Exhale throughout curling action.

PRONE LEG CURL

HIP ADDUCTOR

Joint action

Hip adduction

Prime mover muscles

Hip adductors

Movement path

Rotary

Exercise technique

Sit with hip joints aligned with machine axes of rotation. Place thighs outside appropriately positioned movement pads. Grip handles lightly. Pull movement pads together until they make contact. Return slowly to starting position and repeat.

Technique tips

- Keep back against seat.
- Maintain neutral head position.
- Keep ankles in neutral position.
- Exhale throughout inward action.

HIP ADDUCTOR

A

B

LEG EXERCISES

HIP ABDUCTOR

Joint action

Hip abduction

Prime mover muscles

Hip abductors

Movement path

Rotary

Exercise technique

Sit with hip joints aligned with machine axes of rotation. Place thighs inside movement pads. Grip handles lightly. Pull movement pads as far apart as possible. Return slowly to starting position and repeat.

Technique tips

- Keep back against seat.
- Maintain neutral head position.
- Keep ankles in neutral position.
- Exhale throughout outward action.

HIP ABDUCTOR

A

B

43

LEG PRESS

Joint action

Hip and knee extension

Prime mover muscles

Hamstrings, gluteals, and quadriceps

Movement path

Linear

Exercise technique

Sit with feet evenly placed on footpad, lower legs parallel to floor. Crank seat forward until knees are close to chest and directly behind feet. Grip handles lightly. Push footpad forward until knees are almost fully extended. Return slowly to starting position and repeat.

Technique tips

- Keep back against seat.
- Maintain neutral head position.
- Stop extension short of locking knees.
- It is not necessary to flex knees more than 90 degrees between repetitions.
- Exhale throughout pressing action.

LEG PRESS

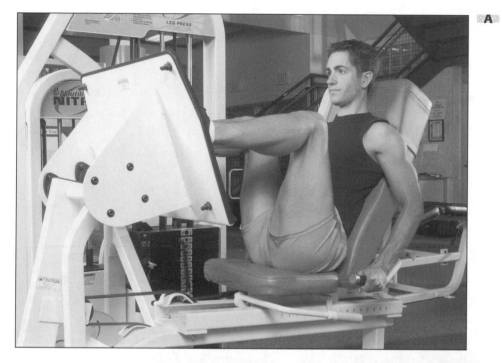

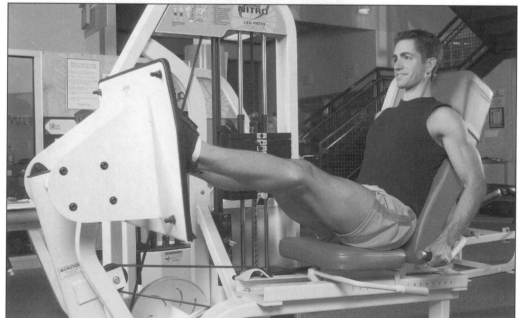

SEATED CALF

Joint action

Ankle extension (plantar flexion)

Prime mover muscles

Gastrocnemius and soleus

Movement path

Rotary

Exercise technique

Sit with knees evenly placed under pads with balls of feet on footbar. Release handle for full movement range. Lift pads upward as far as possible by rising onto toes. Return slowly to starting position and repeat.

Technique tips

- Keep back straight.
- Maintain neutral head position.
- Exhale throughout lifting action.

SEATED CALF

A

B

BARBELL SQUAT

Joint action

Hip extension and knee extension

Prime mover muscles

Hamstrings, gluteals, and quadriceps

Movement path

Linear

Exercise technique

Stand with feet shoulder-width apart or wider and position bar on shoulders while it is on rack. Stand erect to lift bar from rack and step backward. Lower hips downward and backward until thighs are parallel to floor. Return to standing position by extending hips and knees and repeat.

Technique tips

- Keep head up and back straight during downward and upward movement phases.
- Keep feet fully on floor throughout each repetition.
- Keep knees directly above feet throughout each repetition.
- Exhale throughout lifting action.

Note: This exercise must be performed with a spotter to assist if needed.

BARBELL SQUAT

A

B

DUMBBELL LUNGE

Joint action

Hip extension and knee extension

Prime mover muscles

Hamstrings, gluteals, and quadriceps

Movement path

Linear

Exercise technique

Stand with feet shoulder-width apart, holding dumbbells at sides. Step forward with left foot so that left knee is flexed about 90 degrees and right shin is parallel to floor. Return to standing position by extending hips and knees. Repeat, stepping forward with right foot.

Technique tips

- Keep head up and back straight during downward and upward movement phases.
- Step forward far enough so that the knee is directly above the foot.
- Exhale throughout upward action.

DUMBBELL LUNGE

A

B

DUMBBELL STEP-UP

Joint action

Hip extension and knee extension

Prime mover muscles

Hamstrings, gluteals, and quadriceps

Movement path

Linear

Exercise technique

Stand with feet less than shoulder-width apart in front of a sturdy step or box, holding dumbbells at sides. Place left foot on step and lift body to standing position (both feet) on step by extending left hip and knee. Step down with left foot followed by right foot to starting position on floor. Repeat, stepping upward with right foot.

Technique tips

- Keep head up and back straight during downward and upward movement phases.
- Exhale throughout upward action.

DUMBBELL STEP-UP

A

B

BARBELL DEADLIFT

Joint action

Hip extension and knee extension

Prime mover muscles

Hamstrings, gluteals, quadriceps, erector spinae, and upper trapezius

Movement path

Linear

Exercise technique

Stand with feet shoulder-width apart or wider in front of barbell. Flex hips and knees enough to grasp barbell with mixed shoulder-width grip (palms facing each other) and arms straight. Lift barbell to thighs by extending hips and knees. Return slowly to starting position and repeat.

Technique tips

- Keep head up during downward and upward movement phases.
- Keep arms straight throughout each repetition.
- Keep knees directly above feet throughout each repetition.
- Exhale throughout lifting action.

BARBELL DEADLIFT

A

B

BARBELL HEEL RAISE

Joint action

Ankle extension (plantar flexion)

Prime mover muscles

Gastrocnemius and soleus

Movement path

Rotary

Exercise technique

Stand with feet shoulder-width apart on stable elevated surface, holding barbell against front thighs, arms straight. Lift body upward by rising onto toes. Return slowly to starting position and repeat.

Technique tips

- Keep head up and back straight during upward and downward movement phases.

- Keep arms and legs straight throughout each repetition.

- Use maximum movement range by lifting and lowering heels as far as comfortable each repetition.

- Exhale throughout upward action.

BARBELL HEEL RAISE

A

B

CHEST EXERCISES

CHEST CROSS

Joint action

Shoulder horizontal flexion

Prime mover muscles

Pectoralis major and anterior deltoid

Movement path

Rotary

Exercise technique

Sit with shoulder joints aligned with machine axes of rotation. Place elbows against elbow pads and palms against handles. Move elbow pads together as close as possible. Return slowly to starting position and repeat.

Technique tips

- Keep back against seat.
- Maintain neutral head position.
- Lead movements with elbows.
- When positioned properly, upper arms move parallel to floor.
- Exhale throughout inward action.

CHEST CROSS

A

B

CHEST EXERCISES

PEC DEC

Joint action

Shoulder diagonal flexion

Prime mover muscles

Pectoralis major and anterior deltoid

Movement path

Rotary

Exercise technique

Adjust seat to sit with shoulder joints aligned with machine axes of rotation. Partially stand, place arms behind arm pads, and sit in properly aligned position. Move arm pads together as close as possible. Return slowly to starting position and repeat.

Technique tips

- Keep back against seat.
- Maintain neutral head position.
- It is not necessary to raise arms higher than shoulders between repetitions.
- Exhale throughout inward action.

PEC DEC

A

B

CHEST EXERCISES

BENCH PRESS

Joint action

Shoulder horizontal flexion and elbow extension

Prime mover muscles

Pectoralis major, anterior deltoid, and triceps

Movement path

Linear

Exercise technique

Lie with chest directly below handles. Grasp handles slightly wider than shoulders. Press handles upward until elbows are almost fully extended. Return slowly to starting position and repeat.

Technique tips

- Keep head and hips on bench.
- Keep feet on floor or footrest.
- When positioned properly, arms move perpendicular to floor.
- Exhale throughout pressing action.

BENCH PRESS

A

B

INCLINE PRESS

Joint action

Shoulder horizontal flexion and elbow extension

Prime mover muscles

Pectoralis major, anterior deltoid, and triceps

Movement path

Linear

Exercise technique

Sit with shoulders approximately even with handles. Press handles upward until elbows are almost fully extended. Return slowly to starting position and repeat.

Technique tips

- Maintain neutral head position.
- When positioned properly, arms move perpendicular to the floor.
- Exhale throughout pressing action.

INCLINE PRESS

A

B

CHEST EXERCISES

VERTICAL CHEST

Joint action

Shoulder horizontal flexion and elbow extension

Prime mover muscles

Pectoralis major, anterior deltoid, and triceps

Movement path

Linear

Exercise technique

Sit with chest directly behind handles. Press handles forward until elbows are almost fully extended. Return slowly to starting position and repeat.

Technique tips

- Maintain neutral head position.
- When positioned properly, upper arms move approximately parallel to the floor.
- Wide handles place greater emphasis on pectoralis major muscles.
- Narrow handles place greater emphasis on triceps muscles.
- Exhale throughout pressing action.

VERTICAL CHEST

A

B

WEIGHT-ASSISTED BAR DIP

Joint action

Shoulder flexion and elbow extension

Prime mover muscles

Pectoralis major, anterior deltoid, and triceps

Movement path

Linear

Exercise technique

Grip dip bars, place knees on platform and hold straight-arm support position. Lower body until elbows are bent 90 degrees. Press up slowly to straight-arm position and repeat. Remove knees from platform in top position.

Technique tips

- Maintain erect posture.
- Maintain neutral head position.
- Always enter and exit knee platform in top position.
- Exhale throughout pressing action.

WEIGHT-ASSISTED BAR DIP

A

B

CHEST EXERCISES

DUMBBELL BENCH FLY

Joint action

Shoulder horizontal flexion

Prime mover muscles

Pectoralis major and anterior deltoid

Movement path

Rotary

Exercise technique

Lie face-up on flat bench with feet flat on floor. Hold dumbbells above chest with palms facing each other. Lower dumbbells downward and outward until upper arms are approximately parallel to floor. Lift dumbbells upward and inward to starting position and repeat.

Technique tips

- Keep head and hips on bench.
- Keep feet on floor.
- Keep elbows bent throughout exercise.
- When positioned properly, arms move perpendicular to floor.
- Exhale throughout lifting action.

DUMBBELL BENCH FLY

A

B

DUMBBELL INCLINE FLY

Joint action

Shoulder horizontal flexion

Prime mover muscles

Pectoralis major and anterior deltoid

Movement path

Rotary

Exercise technique

Lie face-up on incline bench with feet flat on floor. Hold dumbbells above upper chest with palms facing each other. Lower dumbbells downward and outward until upper arms are approximately parallel to floor. Lift dumbbells upward and inward to starting position and repeat.

Technique tips

- Keep head on bench.
- Keep feet on floor.
- Keep elbows bent throughout exercise.
- When positioned properly, arms move perpendicular to floor.
- Exhale throughout lifting action.

DUMBBELL INCLINE FLY

A

B

CHEST EXERCISES

BARBELL BENCH PRESS

Joint action

Shoulder horizontal flexion and elbow extension

Prime mover muscles

Pectoralis major, anterior deltoid, and triceps

Movement path

Linear

Exercise technique

Lie face-up on flat bench with feet flat on floor. Grasp barbell with shoulder-width or wider grip, lift off rack, and hold directly over chest, arms extended. Lower barbell to thickest part of chest. Press barbell upward to starting position and repeat.

Technique tips

- Keep head and hips on bench.
- Keep feet on floor.
- Lower and lift barbell evenly.
- When positioned properly, arms move perpendicular to floor.
- Exhale throughout lifting action.

Note: This exercise must be performed with a spotter to assist if needed.

BARBELL BENCH PRESS

A

B

CHEST EXERCISES

BARBELL INCLINE PRESS

Joint action

Shoulder horizontal flexion and elbow extension

Prime mover muscles

Pectoralis major, anterior deltoid, and triceps

Movement path

Linear

Exercise technique

Lie face-up on incline bench with feet flat on floor. Grasp barbell with shoulder-width or wider grip, lift off rack, and hold directly over upper chest, arms extended. Lower barbell and stop on or slightly above upper chest. Press barbell upward to starting position and repeat.

Technique tips

- Keep head on bench.
- Keep feet on floor.
- Lower and lift barbell evenly.
- When positioned properly, arms move perpendicular to floor.
- Exhale throughout lifting action.

Note: This exercise must be performed with a spotter to assist if needed.

BARBELL INCLINE PRESS

A

B

BAR DIP

Joint action

Shoulder flexion and elbow extension

Prime mover muscles

Pectoralis major, anterior deltoid, and triceps

Movement path

Linear

Exercise technique

Grip dip bars and hold straight-arm support position. Lower body until elbows are bent 90 degrees. Press up slowly to straight-arm support position and repeat.

Technique tips

- Maintain erect posture.
- Maintain neutral head position.
- Exhale throughout pressing action.

BAR DIP

A

B

UPPER BACK EXERCISES

SUPER PULLOVER

Joint action

Shoulder extension

Prime mover muscles

Latissimus dorsi and teres major

Movement path

Rotary

Exercise technique

Squeeze seat-adjust lever to sit with shoulders in line with machine axis of rotation (red dot). Secure seat belt and press foot lever to position movement pads. Place arms on movement pads, grip crossbar lightly, and stretch arms upward as far as comfortable. Pull arms downward until crossbar contacts midsection. Return slowly to starting position and repeat. After final repetition, press foot lever to remove arms from movement pads.

Technique tips

- Maintain neutral head position.
- Curl trunk forward slightly during pulling movement to provide low back support against seat back.
- Lead movements with elbows.
- Exhale throughout pulling action.

SUPER PULLOVER

A

B

UPPER BACK EXERCISES

COMPOUND ROW

Joint action

Shoulder extension and elbow flexion

Prime mover muscles

Latissimus dorsi, teres major, posterior deltoid, rhomboids, trapezius, and biceps

Movement path

Linear

Exercise technique

Sit so that hands can just reach top of handles. Pull handles backward as far as possible. Return slowly to starting position and repeat.

Technique tips

- Maintain erect posture.
- Maintain neutral head position.
- Keep chest against support pad throughout exercise.

COMPOUND ROW

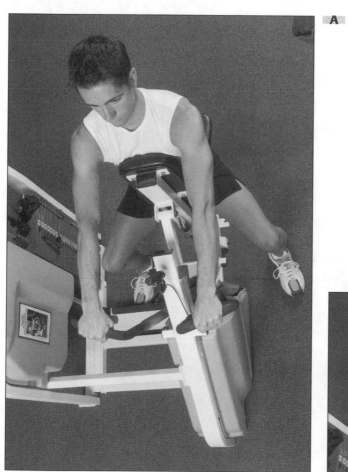

A

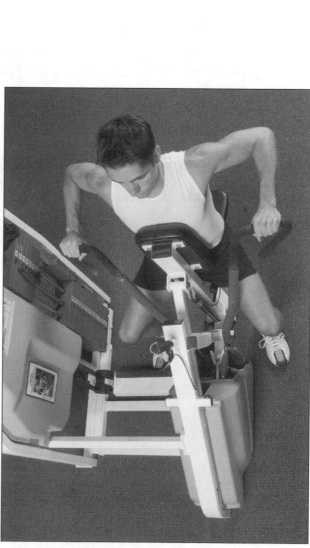

B

UPPER BACK EXERCISES

PULLDOWN

Joint action

Shoulder extension and elbow flexion

Prime mover muscles

Latissimus dorsi, teres major, and biceps

Movement path

Linear

Exercise technique

Adjust seat to just reach handles and secure thighs under roller pads. Pull handles downward below chin level. Return slowly to starting position and repeat.

Technique tips

- Maintain erect posture.
- Maintain neutral head position.
- Palms should generally face each other throughout the exercise movement.
- Exhale throughout pulling action.

PULLDOWN

A

B

UPPER BACK EXERCISES

WEIGHT-ASSISTED CHIN-UP

Joint action

Shoulder extension and elbow flexion

Prime mover muscles

Latissimus dorsi, teres major, and biceps

Movement path

Linear

Exercise technique

Grasp chin bar, place knees on platform, and lower body to full-hang position. Pull body upward until chin is above chin bar. Return slowly to full-hang position and repeat. Remove knees from platform in top position.

Technique tips

- Maintain erect posture.
- Maintain neutral head position.
- Always enter and exit knee platform in top position.
- Shoulder-width grip with palms toward face recommended for best results.
- Exhale throughout pulling action.

WEIGHT-ASSISTED CHIN-UP

A

B

UPPER BACK EXERCISES

DUMBBELL PULLOVER

Joint action

Shoulder extension

Prime mover muscles

Latissimus dorsi, teres major, and triceps

Movement path

Rotary

Exercise technique

Lie face-up on flat bench and hold dumbbell in both hands with arms extended above chest. Lower dumbbell slowly backward and downward behind head as far as comfortable. Lift dumbbell upward and forward to starting position and repeat.

Technique tips

- Keep head and hips on bench at all times.
- Keep arms relatively straight during lifting and lowering movements.
- Exhale throughout lifting action.

DUMBBELL PULLOVER

A

B

DUMBBELL BENT ROW

Joint action

Shoulder extension and elbow flexion

Prime mover muscles

Latissimus dorsi, teres major, posterior deltoid, rhomboids, trapezius, and biceps

Movement path

Linear

Exercise technique

Place left knee and left hand on flat bench to support back parallel to floor. Grasp dumbbell with right hand, arm extended. Pull dumbbell to chest. Return slowly to starting position and repeat.

Technique tips

- Maintain neutral head position.
- Maintain back parallel to floor.
- Elbow near torso places greater emphasis on latissimus dorsi and teres major muscles.
- Elbow away from torso places greater emphasis on posterior deltoid muscle.
- Exhale throughout pulling action.

DUMBBELL BENT ROW

A

B

UPPER BACK EXERCISES

PULLDOWN (WITH BAR)

Joint action

Shoulder extension and elbow flexion

Prime mover muscles

Latissimus dorsi, teres major, and biceps

Movement path

Linear

Exercise technique

Adjust seat to just reach bar and secure thighs under restraining pads. Pull bar downward below chin. Return slowly to starting position and repeat.

Technique tips

- Maintain erect posture.
- Maintain neutral head position.
- Shoulder-width grip with palms toward face recommended for best results.
- Exhale throughout pulling action.

PULLDOWN (WITH BAR)

A

B

UPPER BACK EXERCISES

CHIN-UP

Joint action

Shoulder extension and elbow flexion

Prime mover muscles

Latissimus dorsi, teres major, and biceps

Movement path

Linear

Exercise technique

Grasp chin bar and lower body to full-hang position. Pull body upward until chin is above chin bar. Return slowly to full-hang position and repeat.

Technique tips

- Maintain erect posture.
- Maintain neutral head position.
- Shoulder-width grip with palms toward face recommended for best results.
- Exhale throughout pulling action.

CHIN-UP

A

B

SHOULDER EXERCISES

LATERAL RAISE

Joint action

Shoulder abduction

Prime mover muscles

Deltoids

Movement path

Rotary

Exercise technique

Squeeze seat-adjust lever to sit with shoulders in line with machine axes of rotation (red dots). Place arms against sides inside movement pads. Lift movement pads just above horizontal. Return slowly to starting position and repeat.

Technique tips

- Keep back against seat back.
- Maintain neutral head position.
- Lead movements with elbows.
- Exhale throughout lifting action.

LATERAL RAISE

A

B

SHOULDER EXERCISES

OVERHEAD PRESS

Joint action

Shoulder abduction and elbow extension

Prime mover muscles

Deltoids and triceps

Movement path

Linear

Exercise technique

Sit with shoulders slightly lower than handles. Press handles upward until elbows are almost fully extended. Return slowly to starting position and repeat.

Technique tips

- Keep back against seat back.
- Maintain neutral head position.
- Wide handles place greater emphasis on middle deltoid muscle.
- Narrow handles place greater emphasis on anterior deltoid muscle.
- Exhale throughout pressing action.

OVERHEAD PRESS

A

B

SHOULDER EXERCISES

DUMBBELL LATERAL RAISE

Joint action

Shoulder abduction

Prime mover muscles

Deltoids

Movement path

Rotary

Exercise technique

Stand with feet shoulder-width apart, holding dumbbells in front of torso with elbows bent 90 degrees. Lift dumbbells upward until arms are parallel to floor by rotating shoulder joint through 90 degrees of movement. Return slowly to starting position and repeat.

Technique tips

- Maintain erect posture.
- Maintain neutral head position.
- Maintain 90-degree bend in elbow joint throughout lifting and lowering movements.
- Exhale throughout lifting action.

DUMBBELL LATERAL RAISE

A

B

DUMBBELL PRESS

Joint action

Shoulder abduction and elbow extension

Prime mover muscles

Deltoids and triceps

Movement path

Linear

Exercise technique

Stand with feet shoulder-width apart, holding dumbbells at shoulder level with palms facing forward. Press dumbbells upward until elbows are almost fully extended. Return slowly to starting position and repeat.

Technique tips

- Maintain erect position.
- Maintain neutral head position.
- Dumbbells may be pressed overhead in an alternating manner if desired.
- Exhale throughout pressing action.

DUMBBELL PRESS

A

B

PREACHER CURL

Joint action

Elbow flexion

Prime mover muscles

Biceps

Movement path

Rotary

Exercise technique

Adjust seat to sit with elbows in line with machine axis of rotation (red dot). Partially stand, grip movement bar loosely, and sit in properly aligned position. Curl movement bar upward as far as possible. Return slowly to starting position and repeat. After final repetition, partially stand and lower movement bar to resting position.

Technique tips

- Maintain erect posture.
- Maintain neutral head position.
- It is not necessary to fully extend the elbows between repetitions.
- Exhale throughout curling action.

PREACHER CURL

A

B

BICEPS CURL

Joint action

Elbow flexion

Prime mover muscles

Biceps

Movement path

Rotary

Exercise technique

Adjust seat and seat back to sit with elbows in line with machine axes of rotation (red dots). Partially stand, grip handles loosely, and sit in properly aligned position. Curl handles backward until biceps are fully contracted. Return slowly to starting position and repeat. After final repetition, partially stand and lower handles to resting position.

Technique tips

- Maintain erect posture.
- Maintain neutral head position.
- It is not necessary to fully extend the elbows between repetitions.
- Exhale throughout curling action.

BICEPS CURL

A

B

ARM EXERCISES

LOW TRICEPS EXTENSION

Joint action

Elbow extension

Prime mover muscles

Triceps

Movement path

Rotary

Exercise technique

Adjust back support and seat to sit with elbows in line with machine axis of rotation (red dot). Place sides of hands on movement pads and begin with movement pads beside face. Extend arms downward until triceps are fully contracted. Return slowly to starting position and repeat.

Technique tips

- Keep back against seat back.
- Maintain neutral head position.
- It is not necessary to fully flex the elbows between repetitions.
- Exhale throughout lifting action.

LOW TRICEPS EXTENSION

A

B

ARM EXERCISES

HIGH TRICEPS EXTENSION

Joint action

Elbow extension

Prime mover muscles

Triceps

Movement path

Rotary

Exercise technique

Adjust seat and seat back to sit with elbows in line with machine axes of rotation (red dots). Grip handles loosely and extend arms forward until triceps are fully contracted. Return slowly to starting position and repeat.

Technique tips

- Maintain erect posture.
- Maintain neutral head position.
- It is not necessary to fully flex the elbows between repetitions.
- Exhale throughout lifting action.

HIGH TRICEPS EXTENSION

A

B

ARM EXERCISES

TRICEPS PRESS

Joint action

Shoulder flexion and triceps extension

Prime mover muscles

Pectoralis major, anterior deltoid, and triceps

Movement path

Linear

Exercise technique

Sit with shoulders above handles so that elbows are bent 90 degrees. Secure seat belt. Press handles downward until elbows are almost fully extended. Return slowly to starting position and repeat.

Technique tips

- Elbows away from sides places greater emphasis on pectoralis major muscles.
- Elbows close to sides places greater emphasis on triceps muscles.
- Body may lean slightly forward during exercise performance.
- Exhale throughout pressing action.

TRICEPS PRESS

A

B

DUMBBELL PREACHER CURL

Joint action

Elbow flexion

Prime mover muscles

Biceps

Movement path

Rotary

Exercise technique

Sit on seat with upper arms on preacher bench, palms facing forward. Curl dumbbells upward until biceps are fully contracted. Return slowly to starting position and repeat.

Technique tips

- Maintain erect posture.
- Maintain neutral head position.
- It is not necessary to fully extend the elbows between repetitions.
- Exhale throughout curling action.

DUMBBELL PREACHER CURL

A

B

BARBELL CURL

Joint action

Elbow flexion

Prime mover muscles

Biceps

Movement path

Rotary

Exercise technique

Stand with feet shoulder-width apart and grasp bar with underhand grip, elbows extended. Curl barbell to shoulders. Return slowly to starting position and repeat.

Technique tips

- Maintain erect posture.
- Maintain neutral head position.
- Keep elbows against sides throughout lifting and lowering movements.
- Exhale throughout curling action.

BARBELL CURL

A

B

ARM EXERCISES

TRICEPS PRESSDOWN

Joint action

Elbow extension

Prime mover muscles

Triceps

Movement path

Rotary

Exercise technique

Stand with feet shoulder-width apart in front of pressdown cable. Grasp V-bar with overhand grip, elbows against sides, and hold at chest level. Push V-bar downward until elbows are fully extended. Return slowly to starting position and repeat.

Technique tips

- Maintain erect posture.
- Maintain neutral head position.
- Return V-bar no higher than chest level between repetitions.
- Exhale throughout extending action.

TRICEPS PRESSDOWN

A

B

DUMBBELL OVERHEAD TRICEPS EXTENSION

Joint action

Elbow extension

Prime mover muscles

Triceps

Movement path

Rotary

Exercise technique

Stand with feet shoulder-width apart, grasp dumbbell with both hands, and hold with arms extended overhead. Lower dumbbell behind head until elbows are fully flexed. Extend arms upward until elbows are fully extended and repeat.

Technique tips

- Maintain erect posture.
- Maintain neutral head position.
- Keep upper arms perpendicular to floor throughout lifting and lowering movements.
- Exhale throughout lifting action.

DUMBBELL OVERHEAD TRICEPS EXTENSION

A

B

DUMBBELL TRICEPS KICKBACK

Joint action

Elbow extension

Prime mover muscles

Triceps

Movement path

Rotary

Exercise technique

Place left knee and left hand on flat bench to support back parallel to floor. Hold dumbbell in right hand with elbow bent 90 degrees and pressed firmly against hip. Lift dumbbell backward and upward until elbow is fully extended. Return slowly to starting position and repeat.

Technique tips

- Maintain neutral head position.
- Keep back parallel to floor throughout exercise.
- Keep elbow firmly pressed against hip throughout lifting and lowering movements.
- Exhale throughout lifting action.

DUMBBELL TRICEPS KICKBACK

A

B

ABDOMINAL CRUNCH

Joint action

Trunk flexion

Prime mover muscles

Rectus abdominis and hip flexors

Movement path

Rotary

Exercise technique

Adjust seat to sit with navel in line with red dot. Anchor feet under adjustable foot pads if desired. Place elbows on movement pads and grip handles lightly. Pull chest toward hips in crunch movement until abdominal muscles are fully contracted. Return slowly to starting position and repeat.

Technique tips

- Keep upper back against seat back.
- Keep head neutral or slightly forward.
- Feet in front of foot pads places greater emphasis on abdominal muscles.
- Feet under foot pads places greater emphasis on hip flexor muscles.
- Exhale throughout crunching action.

ABDOMINAL CRUNCH

A

B

MIDSECTION EXERCISES

LOW BACK EXTENSION

Joint action

Trunk extension

Prime mover muscles

Erector spinae

Movement path

Rotary

Exercise technique

Adjust seat to sit with navel in line with red dot. Position foot pad so knees are slightly higher than hips. Secure both seat belts across thighs. Push movement pad backward until low back muscles are fully contracted. Return slowly to starting position and repeat.

Technique tips

- Keep hips against seat back.
- Maintain neutral head position.
- Fold arms across chest.
- Exhale throughout lifting action.

LOW BACK EXTENSION

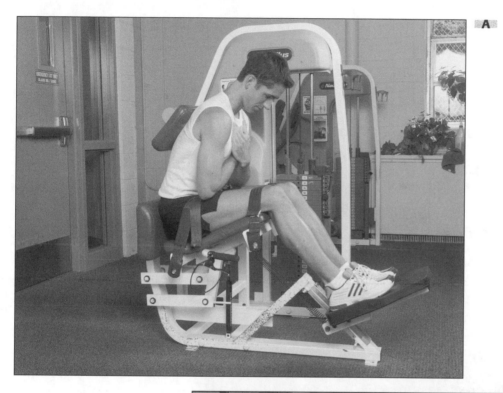

A

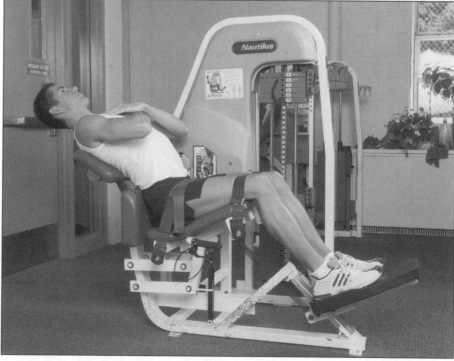

B

ROTARY TORSO

Joint action

Trunk rotation

Prime mover muscles

External obliques and internal obliques

Movement path

Rotary

Exercise technique

Sit with hips against seat ridge. Place arms behind arm pads. Turn torso clockwise until oblique muscles are fully contracted; return slowly and repeat. Adjust seat position. Turn torso counterclockwise until oblique muscles are fully contracted; return slowly and repeat.

Technique tips

- Maintain erect posture.
- Maintain neutral head position.
- When hips are stabilized, the trunk has a relatively short rotation range (about 70 degrees).
- Exhale throughout turning and lifting action.

ROTARY TORSO

A

B

KNEE LIFT

Joint action

Hip flexion

Prime mover muscles

Rectus femoris, iliacus, psoas, and rectus abdominis

Movement path

Rotary

Exercise technique

Grip dip bars and hold straight-arm support position. Lift both knees upward until thighs are parallel to floor. Return slowly to starting position and repeat.

Technique tips

- Maintain erect posture.
- Maintain neutral head position.
- Exhale throughout lifting action.

KNEE LIFT

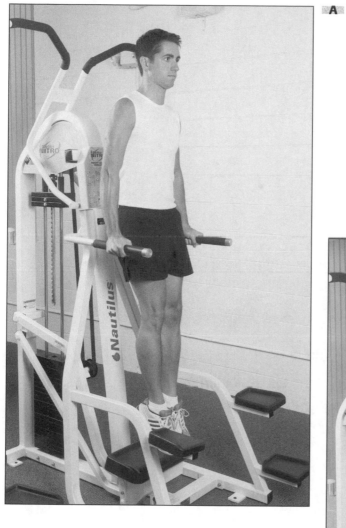

A

B

TRUNK CURL

Joint action

Trunk flexion

Prime mover muscles

Rectus abdominis

Movement path

Rotary

Exercise technique

Lie face-up with knees flexed, feet flat on floor, and hands clasped loosely behind head. Lift shoulders off floor about 30 degrees until abdominal muscles are fully contracted. Return slowly to starting position and repeat.

Technique tips

- Maintain neutral head position throughout.
- Keep arms straight throughout lifting and lowering movements.
- Exhale throughout upward actions.

TRUNK CURL

A

B

MIDSECTION EXERCISES

TRUNK EXTENSION

Joint action

Trunk extension

Prime mover muscles

Erector spinae

Movement path

Rotary

Exercise technique

Lie face-down on floor with hands folded under chin. Raise chest off floor about 30 degrees until low back muscles are fully contracted. Return slowly to starting position and repeat.

Technique tips

- Maintain neutral head position.
- Keep hips and feet on floor at all times; secure feet under sturdy anchor object if necessary.
- Exhale throughout lifting action.

TRUNK EXTENSION

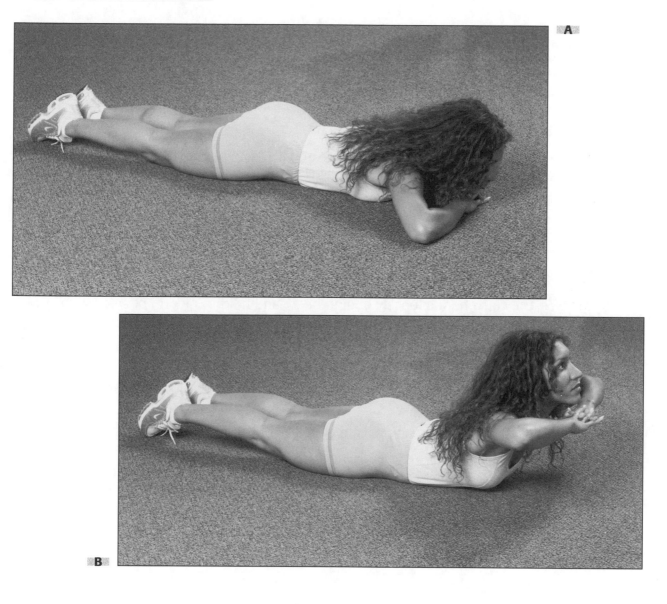

A

B

MIDSECTION EXERCISES

TWISTING KNEE-LIFT TRUNK CURL

Joint action

Trunk flexion, trunk rotation, hip flexion and extension, and knee flexion and extension

Prime mover muscles

Rectus abdominis, obliques, hip flexors and extensors, and knee flexors and extensors

Movement path

Rotary and linear

Exercise technique

Lie face-up, clasp hands loosely behind head, and hold trunk curl position with lower back pressed against floor. Lift both feet a few inches off floor and alternately bring knees backward and forward. Alternately twist torso from side to side, attempting to touch right elbow to left knee and left elbow to right knee.

Technique tips

- Maintain neutral head position throughout trunk twisting movements.
- Keep lower back pressed against floor throughout exercise.
- It is not necessary to fully extend knees in forward leg movements.
- Breathe continuously throughout exercise.

TWISTING KNEE-LIFT TRUNK CURL

A

B

NECK EXERCISES

4-WAY NECK

Joint action

Neck flexion, neck extension, and neck lateral flexion

Prime mover muscles

Sternocleidomastoid, upper trapezius, and levator scapulae

Movement path

Rotary

Exercise technique

Sit with face against movement pad. Grasp handles loosely. Push movement pad forward as far as possible. Return slowly to starting position and repeat. Sit with rear of head against movement pad. Grasp handles loosely. Push movement pad backward as far as possible. Return slowly to starting position and repeat. Sit with side of head against movement pad. Grasp handles loosely. Push movement pad sideward as far as possible. Return slowly to starting position and repeat. Sit with other side of head against movement pad. Grasp handles loosely. Push movement pad sideward as far as possible. Return slowly to starting position and repeat.

Technique tips

- Maintain erect posture.
- Keep torso in contact with restraining pad.
- Exhale throughout lifting actions.

4-WAY NECK

BARBELL SHOULDER SHRUG

Joint action

Shoulder elevation

Prime mover muscles

Upper trapezius

Movement path

Rotary

Exercise technique

Stand with feet shoulder-width apart and hold barbell with overhand grip, arms fully extended. Lift barbell upward a few inches by elevating shoulders toward head. Return slowly to starting position and repeat.

Technique tips

- Maintain erect posture.
- Maintain neutral head position.
- Keep arms straight throughout lifting and lowering movements.
- Exhale throughout lifting actions.

BARBELL SHOULDER SHRUG

A

B

High-Intensity Strength Training

Congratulations! By this point you should have attained a fairly high level of strength fitness. However, you may also experience a training plateau; that is, you are working just as hard but making few strength gains. Although lack of progress may be discouraging, it is simply a sign that you should change your exercise program. Of course, everyone has different genetic potential for muscular development, so you should approach advanced training in a sensible manner.

The three best approaches for overcoming strength plateaus are to choose new exercises, change workout protocol, or increase training intensity. This chapter discusses all three of these methods of advanced training.

Choose New Exercises

A sound recommendation for achieving further strength gains is to select new training exercises. For example, if you are not progressing in the bench press exercise, simply substitute the incline press exercise. The slightly different movement pattern still targets the pectoralis major muscle but activates different muscle fibers and produces a new stimulus for strength development.

Periodically changing training exercises is an excellent means of preventing both boredom and strength plateaus. However, you should stay with a given exercise protocol long enough to maximize muscle response. Spend at least one month with a specific exercise program to allow your muscles time to adapt to the new training stimulus.

Change Workout Protocol

In addition to choosing new training exercises, you should systematically vary your workout procedures. This is called *periodization* and involves changing your exercise resistance and repetitions scheme. For example, during the first month, you may complete 12 to 16 repetitions with relatively light resistance. During the second month, you may do 8 to 12 repetitions with moderate weight loads. During the third month, you may perform 4 to 8 repetitions with relatively heavy resistance.

Periodically changing the resistance–repetitions relationship varies the muscle fiber activation pattern and provides a new stimulus for strength development. Just be sure to give each training program enough time to be productive. For continuity, try not to change strength training protocol more often than every four weeks.

Increase Training Intensity

One way to make your workouts more demanding is to perform more exercises for each major muscle group. Another means of increasing workout volume is to complete more sets of each exercise. Competitive bodybuilders have traditionally taken this track, training two to four hours a day, six days a week. But recently, because of time limitations and overtraining injuries, many strength enthusiasts have taken a different approach to advanced workouts called high-intensity strength training. These time-efficient exercise procedures have produced excellent results for people of various ages and abilities, including champion bodybuilders and professional football teams.

The basic premise of high-intensity strength training is that you can exercise hard or you can exercise long, but you can't exercise hard for long. The key to effective high-intensity strength training is to put more effort into each set rather than to put more sets into your workout. This type of training emphasizes the exercise intensity instead of the exercise duration. Just keep in mind that more demanding exercise sessions require more time for tissue recovery and muscle building. For best results, you should perform high-intensity strength training no more than twice a week.

Consider the difference between multiple-set and high-intensity strength training. Because the motor unit activation pattern is essentially the same for a specific exercise, repeat sets fatigue the same muscle fibers again and again rather than stimulating additional muscle fibers.

For example, if you perform 10 leg extensions to temporary muscle fatigue with 75 percent of your maximum resistance, you fatigue or stimulate about 25 percent of the quadriceps muscle fibers. If you rest two minutes and repeat this procedure, you again fatigue or stimulate the same 25 percent of the quadriceps muscle fibers.

In contrast, let's say you perform 10 leg extensions to temporary muscle fatigue with 75 percent of your maximum resistance, which fatigues or stimulates 25 percent of the quadriceps muscle fibers. But instead of stopping, you immediately reduce the resistance by 10 to 20 percent and complete a few additional repetitions. Doing a few post-fatigue repetitions with a reduced resistance fatigues or stimulates more muscle fibers for a greater strength-building effect. In other words, when you reduce the weight load and perform an extended exercise set, you experience two progressive levels of muscle fatigue, which provides a greater stimulus for strength development.

Extending the Exercise Set

There are three standard high-intensity procedures for extending the exercise set and enhancing the strength-building stimulus. These techniques are known as breakdown training, assisted training, and pre-exhaustion training. Here is how they work.

Breakdown Training

You now know that one means of fatiguing or stimulating more muscle fibers is to perform a few additional repetitions with slightly less resistance upon reaching temporary muscle fatigue. This high-intensity exercise technique is typically called breakdown training because you break down the resistance to accommodate your momentarily reduced muscle strength.

As a general rule, reach temporary muscle fatigue with your standard exercise weight load (about 8 to 12 repetitions), then quickly reduce the resistance by approximately 10 to 20 percent. This should permit you to complete about two to four additional repetitions, thereby reaching a second level of muscle fatigue or stimulus within the anaerobic energy system (less than 90 seconds). For example, you may perform 10 lateral raises to fatigue with 10-pound dumbbells. Quickly exchange these for 8-pound dumbbells and complete four more repetitions to a second level of muscle fatigue.

Researchers recently examined the effects of breakdown training on strength development in beginning exercisers.[1] All 45 subjects performed standard strength training (one set of 8 to 12 repetitions to fatigue) on 11 Nautilus machines for the first four weeks of the study. During the second four weeks, half of the subjects continued their standard training, while the other half performed breakdown training on two of the machines (seated leg curl and abdominal). The participants who performed breakdown training experienced 40 percent more strength development during the eight-week exercise period. The standard training produced an 18-pound improvement in the two exercises, while the breakdown training produced a 25-pound strength gain.

Because breakdown training reduces the resistance at the point of muscle fatigue, it is a safe exercise technique, as well as an effective one for beginning participants. However, to determine if breakdown training can produce further improvement in advanced exercisers, we conducted another study with 11 well-trained men and women. After just six weeks of breakdown training, they increased their average exercise resistance by 14 pounds. In addition, they performed 1.5 more chin-ups and 2.5 more bar dips after breakdown training even though they did not practice these exercises during the study period. That is, breakdown training produced significant improvements in both weight-stack and body weight exercises in previously plateaued participants.

Assisted Training

Assisted training is another high-intensity training procedure for fatiguing or stimulating more muscle fibers by extending the exercise set. Like breakdown training, assisted training allows you to complete a few additional repetitions with reduced resistance when you reach temporary muscle fatigue. However, in assisted training the weight load remains the same for post-fatigue repetitions. Your assistant helps you lift the weight load but allows you to lower the weight load on your own. This works well because muscles are about 40 percent stronger in lowering movements (negative muscle actions) than in lifting movements (positive muscle actions).

Nonetheless, as you further fatigue the target muscles, the lowering movements become increasingly more difficult. You should end the extended exercise set at the point where you can no longer control the lowering movement. When performed properly, this typically occurs within two to four assisted repetitions, enabling you to reach both concentric and eccentric muscle fatigue within the anaerobic energy system (under 90 seconds).

We also studied the effects of assisted training on strength gains in beginning exercisers.[2] All 42 subjects performed standard strength training (one set of 8 to 12 repetitions to fatigue) on 11 Nautilus machines for the first four weeks of the study. During the next four weeks, half of the subjects continued their standard training, while the other half performed assisted training on two of the machines (seated leg curl and abdominal). The participants who performed assisted training experienced 45 percent greater strength gains during the eight-week exercise period. The standard training produced a 20-pound strength improvement in the two exercises, while the assisted training produced a 29-pound strength gain.

Like breakdown training, assisted training reduces the resistance at the point of muscle fatigue, which makes it a safe and productive exercise procedure for beginning participants. To see if assisted training can further enhance strength development in advanced exercisers, we completed another study with 15 well-conditioned men and women. After just five weeks of assisted training, they increased their average exercise resistance by 11 pounds. They also performed 1.4 more chin-ups and 4.5 more bar dips after assisted training even though they did not practice these exercises during the study period. In other words, assisted training produced significant improvements in both weight-stack and body weight exercises in previously plateaued participants.

Pre-Exhaustion Training

A third method of extending the exercise set in a high-intensity manner is pre-exhaustion training. If you like to do more than one set of exercise for the target muscle group, you should definitely try the pre-exhaustion procedure. Pre-exhaustion training begins with a rotary (curved path) exercise to fatigue the target muscle, followed immediately by a linear (straight path) exercise that brings in fresh assisting muscles to further fatigue the target muscle.

The first set of rotary exercise should cause muscle fatigue within 60 seconds (about 10 repetitions), and the follow-up set of linear exercise should cause muscle fatigue within 30 seconds (about 5 repetitions). The successive exercises for the same target muscle should provide two progressive levels of muscle stimulus within the anaerobic energy system (90 seconds).

For example, when you perform two sets of 10 bench presses with the same resistance, you activate the same pectoralis major muscle fibers twice. This procedure increases the exercise duration but does not necessarily increase the exercise intensity. That is, you work the same muscle fibers more rather than work more muscle fibers.

Instead, perform a set of chest crosses (10 repetitions) followed immediately by a set of bench presses (5 repetitions). The chest cross is a rotary exercise that largely isolates the pectoralis major muscle. When the target muscle fatigues, you can no longer continue this exercise. But if you immediately perform the bench press, a linear exercise that uses both the pre-fatigued pectoralis major and the fresh triceps, you can push the target muscle (pectoralis major) to a deeper level of fatigue or stimulus (see figure 5.1, a and b).

■ **Figure 5.1** *(a)* A rotary exercise effectively exhausts the target muscles. *(b)* A linear exercise uses assisting muscles to help further fatigue target muscles after a rotary exercise.

Basically, the different movement patterns of the chest cross and bench press activate different muscle fibers, and assistance from the fresh triceps muscle permits the fatigued pectoralis major to do even more work for better strength-building benefits. Table 5.1 presents several pairs of rotary and linear exercises that provide pre-exhaustion training for most of the major muscle groups.

Table 5.1 Examples of Pre-Exhaustion Exercises

Muscle group	Rotary exercise	Linear exercise
Quadriceps	Leg extension	Leg press
Hamstrings	Leg curl	Leg press
Pectoralis major	Pec dec	Vertical chest
Latissimus dorsi	Pullover	Lat pulldown
Deltoids	Lateral raise	Overhead press
Biceps	Biceps curl	Assisted chin-up
Triceps	High triceps extension	Assisted bar dip

Extending the Exercise Repetition— Slow Training

Slow training is a form of high-intensity training that produces a greater strength stimulus by extending each exercise repetition. By performing each repetition more slowly, you reduce the role of momentum and enhance both muscle tension and muscle force production. The standard slow training method, developed in 1982 by Ken Hutchins and called Super Slow® exercise, uses a 10-second lifting movement (positive muscle action) and a 4-second lowering movement (negative muscle action) for a 14-second repetition. Four to six repetitions are recommended to fatigue the target muscles within the anaerobic energy system (4×14 seconds = 56 seconds; 6×14 seconds = 84 seconds). When doing slow-speed strength exercise, be sure to breathe continuously throughout every repetition; never hold your breath. In spite of being tough, tensive, and tedious to perform, slow training has proved to be a productive procedure for increasing muscle strength in both beginning and advanced exercisers. For example, in one study 147 subjects were divided into a standard training group (8 to 12 repetitions at 7 seconds each) and a slow training group (4 to 6 repetitions at 14 seconds each). The slow training participants gained 50 percent more strength (25.5 pounds versus 17.0 pounds) over the two-month training period.[3]

Comparison of High-Intensity and Standard Training

A recent study examined the effects of various high-intensity techniques and standard training on advanced exercisers whose strength had plateaued.[4] The 22 subjects performed some exercises with standard training (one set of 8 to 12 repetitions, 2 seconds lifting and 4 seconds lowering) and other exercises with various high-intensity training techniques. These included breakdown training (3 post-fatigue reps with reduced resistance), assisted training (3 post-fatigue reps with manual assistance), slow positive-emphasis training (10 seconds lifting and 4 seconds lowering), and slow negative-emphasis training (4 seconds lifting and 10 seconds lowering). All of the exercise procedures produced significant improvements in muscle strength over the six-week training period, including standard training supervised by an instructor (see figure 5.2). Apparently, working with an instructor encourages better training technique and elicits greater exercise effort. Even so, each of the high-intensity training techniques produced more strength gain than standard training.

Combined High-Intensity Training Program

Perhaps the most successful system of high-intensity strength training is a six-week program that includes all of the advanced techniques. As presented in table 5.2, the experienced exercisers performed breakdown training during the first week, assisted training during the second week, slow positive-emphasis training during the third week, slow negative-emphasis training during the fourth week, pre-exhaustion training during the fifth week, and their preferred high-intensity training technique during the final week. They worked all of their major muscle groups in 30-minute sessions on Mondays and Fridays with an instructor. The 48 subjects increased their exercise weight loads by 17.8 pounds, increased their lean (muscle) weight by 2.5 pounds, and decreased their fat weight by 3.3 pounds.

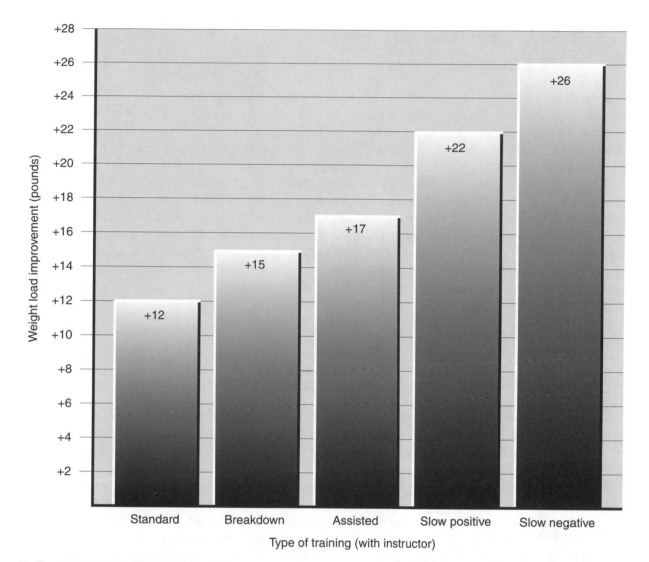

Figure 5.2 Strength improvements for previously plateaued individuals after six weeks of training using different exercise techniques.

Table 5.2 Combined High-Intensity Strength Training Program Components

Week	Exercise technique	Description
One	Breakdown training	8 to 12 reps to fatigue, then 2 to 4 post-fatigue reps with 10 to 20% less resistance
Two	Assisted training	8 to 12 reps to fatigue, then 2 to 4 post-fatigue reps with manual assistance
Three	Slow-positive training	4 to 6 reps to fatigue, taking 10 sec. for lifting movements and 4 sec. for lowering movements
Four	Slow-negative training	4 to 6 reps to fatigue, taking 4 sec. for lifting movements and 10 sec. for lowering movements
Five	Pre-exhaustion training	About 10 reps to fatigue with rotary exercise followed by about 5 reps to fatigue with linear exercise for the target muscle group
Six	Personal preference	Repeat of favorite high-intensity training technique

Comparison of High-Intensity and Boot-Camp Training

Our most interesting study, performed for the United States Navy, compared a 30-minute per session high-intensity strength training program with a 60-minute per session boot-camp exercise program.[5] Both groups trained twice a week for a period of five weeks. The high-intensity training consisted of a pre-exhaustion protocol and assisted repetitions, whereas the boot-camp training involved body weight exercises such as push-ups and sit-ups.

All 34 previously trained participants improved their strength performance in the assessment exercises (chin-ups and bar dips), even though neither group practiced these exercises during the study period. However, the high-intensity trainees attained significantly more chin-ups and bar dips, as well as large increases in their weight-stack exercises. Psychological surveys completed before and after the five-week exercise programs showed no indications of burnout among the high-intensity trainees. It was therefore concluded that the relatively brief high-intensity strength training protocol is an effective and efficient alternative to the relatively long and redundant boot-camp training procedures.

Summary

On reaching a strength plateau, you may continue to attain muscle development by choosing new exercises, changing workout protocol, or increasing training intensity. The latter approach has produced excellent results for exercise enthusiasts at all levels of strength fitness. High-intensity strength training typically involves extending the exercise set (as in breakdown, assisted, and pre-exhaustion procedures) or extending the exercise repetition (as in slow-speed training).

In addition to being extremely effective, high-intensity strength training is very time-efficient. Participants typically train only 30 minutes each session and perform just two workouts a week. This type of high-effort exercise produces a greater strength-building stimulus but requires more time for muscle remodeling between training sessions.

Training for Cardiovascular Endurance

When you think about endurance training, are you haunted by images of yourself, gaunt and exhausted, dragging over miles of hot and dusty (or maybe cold and snowy) roads? For many of us who don't care about being ultrathin or having exceptional athletic stamina, endurance exercise may seem unpleasant. But in the next few chapters you will see that endurance exercise need not be boring or painful. A variety of aerobic activities and exercise equipment can add pep to your program. And even if your workouts are already challenging, you will find that the results are well worth the effort. To maximize your physical capacity and functional ability as well as reduce the risk of overuse injuries, be sure to read this chapter and the next chapter before beginning your endurance training. You should find that cardiovascular-enhancing exercise can be time-efficient and enjoyable if approached in an appropriate manner.

Benefits of Endurance Exercise

Properly performed endurance training has many physiological benefits. Unfortunately, some fitness enthusiasts have done too much aerobic exercise and have suffered the consequences of various overuse injuries. When you balance your training program, however, you should experience better aerobic fitness and enhanced cardiovascular health as well as injury-free exercise experiences. The best approach to endurance exercise is performing enough aerobic activity to promote cardiovascular benefits but not enough to cause musculoskeletal overuse problems. Let's look more closely at the well-documented reasons that endurance exercise is so important to a healthy lifestyle.

Physical Capacity

The most obvious outcome of regular endurance exercise is the ability to do more vigorous aerobic activity for longer periods. If you are out of shape, you may find it difficult at first to complete even five minutes of light aerobic activity. But as you gradually increase the activity demands, your body adapts and you can exercise at a faster pace for a longer time. Your greater capacity for walking, running, cycling, skating, rowing, and stepping makes endurance exercise a worthwhile endeavor.

Cardiovascular Health

Because heart disease accounts for almost half of all deaths in the United States and a substantial percentage of deaths elsewhere, many of us are concerned about our cardiovascular health.[1] One of the best ways to avoid cardiovascular illness is to develop and maintain a high level of aerobic fitness. Sedentary people have about twice the risk of heart disease as physically active people.[2] Actually, inactivity increases your risk of heart disease just as much as high blood pressure, high blood cholesterol, or cigarette smoking.[3] But even if you have one or more of these risk factors, being in good physical condition can reduce the risk of a heart attack, as shown in figure 6.1.[4] Perhaps even more important, people in poor physical condition have more than three times the risk of death from heart disease and other causes as people with high fitness levels.[5]

To improve your cardiovascular fitness, you need to perform at least 20 minutes of aerobic activity on three nonconsecutive days a week.[6] This is a reasonable time commitment in exchange for enjoying a more active lifestyle and better cardiovascular health.

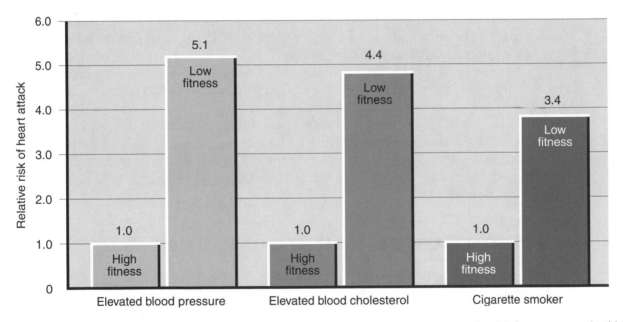

■ **Figure 6.1** Relative risk of heart attack for male public safety officers with cardiovascular risk factors categorized by fitness level.

Reprinted, by permission, from Peters, Cady, Bischoff et al., 1983, "Physical fitness and subsequent myocardial infarction in healthy workers," *JAMA* 249:3052-3056.

Cardiovascular Function

Many cardiovascular benefits result from regular endurance exercise.[7] These positive physiological changes take place in the heart, the circulatory system, and the blood (see table 6.1). Endurance exercise increases the heart's stroke volume and decreases heart rate, making the heart a stronger pump. A greater stroke volume

Table 6.1   Benefits of Cardiovascular Adaptations to Regular Endurance Exercise

1. The heart becomes a stronger pump:
- Stroke volume increases (heart pumps more blood each beat).
- Heart rate decreases (heart beats less frequently).
- Cardiac output increases (pumping capacity improves).

2. The circulatory system becomes more efficient in function:
- Size of blood vessels increases (more blood-carrying capacity).
- Number of blood vessels increases (better blood distribution).
- Tone of blood vessels increases (better blood control).

3. The blood becomes a better transporter:
- Blood volume increases (more transporting capacity).
- Number and mass of red blood cells increase (more oxygen-carrying capacity).
- Platelet stickiness decreases (reduced risk of blood clots).

Data from Fox, S.M., J.P. Naughton, and P.A. Gorman. 1972. Physical activity and cardiovascular health. *Modern Concepts of Cardiovascular Health* 41: 20.

enables the heart to pump more blood every time it beats. A slower heart rate allows the heart to rest longer and to fill more completely with blood between beats.

After several weeks of regular endurance exercise, you should have a reduced resting heart rate. When you consider that an untrained heart beats about 75 times per minute and a trained heart beats about 55 times per minute, the difference is almost 30,000 beats per day! And that means a lot less wear and tear on your most important muscle.

The circulatory system responds to endurance exercise by becoming more efficient. Blood vessels increase in size, number, and tone. Larger blood vessels carry more blood to the working muscles, including the heart. More blood vessels distribute blood better within the working muscles, including the heart. Toned blood vessels respond better to the body's physical demands, reducing blood flow to inactive areas and increasing blood flow to the working muscles as needed. These circulatory system changes may reduce resting blood pressure and enhance cardiovascular function.

Endurance exercise also changes your blood for the better. First, regular aerobic activity increases blood volume, expanding its transporting capacity. Second, it increases the number and size of the red blood cells, enhancing the blood's oxygen-carrying capacity. Third, endurance exercise decreases stickiness among blood platelets, reducing the risk of blood clots.

Although many other cardiovascular improvements result from aerobic activity, learning about these key benefits should encourage you to do some endurance training. Exercise that makes the heart a stronger pump, the circulatory system more efficient, and the blood a better transporter is certainly worth the effort.

Health Benefits

Statistics show that we are all at risk when it comes to cardiovascular disease. Therefore, we should make some effort to improve our chances of good health and long life. The most significant coronary risk factors include high blood pressure, high blood cholesterol, cigarette smoking, obesity, glucose intolerance, and psychological stress. Fortunately, regular endurance exercise may help in all of these areas.

Let's start with high blood pressure. Regular endurance exercise effectively reduces both systolic and diastolic blood pressure. This is true for endurance exercise alone and in combination with strength training.[8,9,10]

Elevated blood cholesterol levels may also be lowered slightly by regular endurance training. More important, endurance exercise has consistently resulted in better ratios of good cholesterol (HDL) to bad cholesterol (LDL), which leads to more desirable lipid profiles.[11]

Although aerobic activity does not automatically cause a person to stop smoking, it may influence smoking behavior. At least one study has demonstrated that those who exercise are less likely to smoke than those who don't exercise.[12] Smoking and endurance activity are certainly incompatible behaviors, especially if one exercises regularly.

More than one-third of adult Americans are classified as obese.[13] In addition to being a cardiovascular risk factor itself, obesity is closely associated with other coronary problems. Although dieting can reduce body fat, it also has the undesirable effect of reducing lean tissue. The best fat loss and body composition changes result when you combine dieting with exercise.[14,15] As presented in chapter 2, you can achieve the best body composition by doing strength and endurance exercise. After eight weeks of strength and endurance training, more than 300 adult participants averaged 3 pounds more muscle and 8.5 pounds less fat, for an 11.5-pound improvement in body composition.[16] Without a doubt, regular endurance exercise can play a significant role in reducing body fat.

Glucose intolerance is associated with insulin resistance in our body tissues, which may lead to type 2 diabetes and heart disease. Fortunately, type 2 diabetes responds favorably to endurance training. Exercise sessions appear to decrease insulin resistance and increase glucose utilization, lessening the risk of glucose intolerance problems.[17]

Psychological stress also contributes to cardiovascular risk.[18] Although research has not proven the positive effects of endurance exercise on psychological stress, most physiologists, psychologists, and fitness enthusiasts agree that physical activity does a good job of reducing the tensions created by daily living.

Lifestyle Benefits

You should notice some important lifestyle benefits from regular aerobic activity, including improved sleep, digestion, and elimination.[7] In addition, people who engage in endurance training often report higher levels of energy, not only for performing their exercise sessions but also for doing other physical activities such as gardening, golf, tennis, cycling, and skiing (see figure 6.2).

Because the heart functions as the fuel pump for the body, a well-conditioned cardiovascular system enhances the energy supply to the muscles. This helps the muscles work better and longer, with less effort and faster recovery. When you combine strength and endurance exercise, the improvements in both muscular and cardiovascular fitness make a remarkable difference in your physical capacity. You may wonder how you were able to function adequately before you became fit.

Endurance Training Options

Now let's look at the many training activities available for designing a workout program. The most popular indoor endurance exercises include treadmill walking and jogging, stationary cycling, and using stepping and rowing machines. Outside the workout room, running, bicycling, swimming, and in-line skating are among the favorites.

In addition to a variety of exercise activities, you can choose from four endurance training methods. The first and most common exercise procedure is steady pace training. The second and most productive exercise procedure is interval training. The third and most comprehensive exercise procedure is cross-training. The fourth and most individualized exercise procedure is known as fartlek training.

■ **Figure 6.2** Cardiovascular fitness is not only terrific for your body but is enjoyable as well!

Steady Pace Training

Most people prefer steady pace training because it involves a consistent and comfortable exercise effort. For instance, you may find it convenient to walk at a specific speed, such as 3.5 miles per hour. This facilitates a steady heart rate response at a given training level for safe and effective endurance exercise sessions. Walking at this pace may raise your heart rate to the appropriate conditioning level, which will be discussed in chapter 7. As you become more fit, you may need to increase your pace to four miles per hour to produce the same training effect.

Steady pace training should not be too easy or too difficult. Make it vigorous enough to stimulate the cardiovascular system but not so strenuous that it is uncomfortable or unpleasant. As a rule, if you are able to converse in short sentences during steady pace training, you are probably exercising at an appropriate (moderate) effort level.

Interval Training

Interval training divides an endurance exercise session into harder and easier segments. For example, you may be able to run four miles at a 9.5-minute-per-mile pace, but you would like to improve to a 9-minute-per-mile pace. Try alternating harder and easier mile segments for the four-mile distance. That is, run the first mile in 9 minutes, the second mile in 10 minutes, the third mile in 9 minutes, and the fourth mile in 10 minutes.

Although your total running time is the same, the effort you put into your workout and the benefits you gain will be greater in the interval training session.

This occurs because the 9-minute-mile segments place higher demands on the cardiovascular system, while the 10-minute-mile segments provide recovery intervals, helping you to maintain a desirable overall heart rate response throughout the workout. Interval training provides better cardiovascular conditioning while preparing the body for a faster running pace.

Another physiological advantage of interval training is that it provides more than one cardiovascular stimulus per training session. Each high-effort training interval has a positive impact on your heart's stroke volume, which helps develop a greater blood pumping capacity.

A psychological advantage of interval training is the faster than normal training pace. Although the high-effort segments may be relatively brief, they demonstrate greater performance potential, making the usual training pace seem a little less demanding by comparison.

The concept of interval training is fairly simple, yet the training options allow considerable personalization. Several interval training variations are possible as you progress to higher levels of cardiovascular fitness:

1. Increase the exercise effort required during the harder intervals.
2. Increase the exercise effort required during the easier intervals.
3. Increase the length of the harder intervals.
4. Decrease the length of the easier intervals.
5. Increase the number of hard and easy intervals that you complete during a training session.

Cross-Training

Cross-training is another approach to endurance exercise. While interval training alternates harder and easier segments of the same exercise, cross-training combines two or more exercise activities. For example, a 30-minute cross-training session may include 10 minutes of recumbent cycling, 10 minutes of stepping, and 10 minutes of jogging. You may do cross-training exercises at a moderate pace or use higher- and lower-effort intervals throughout the workout. Many endurance athletes cross-train during the off-season to maintain their cardiovascular fitness and avoid overuse injuries.

The advantages of cross-training are twofold. Psychologically, by frequently changing the exercises, you are less likely to experience boredom during your training sessions. Physiologically, the cardiovascular system receives a training stimulus throughout the entire exercise session as long as you perform each activity with at least moderate effort. And by using different muscle groups in different activities, you both increase the general conditioning effect and decrease the risk of overuse injuries. For example, cycling emphasizes the quadriceps muscles, jogging emphasizes the hamstring muscles, and stepping targets the quadriceps and calf muscles.

If you prefer to spend an entire exercise session on a single activity, you can apply cross-training on a week-by-week basis. For example, you may do 30 minutes of cycling on Monday, 30 minutes of stepping on Wednesday, and 30 minutes of jogging on Friday. Once again, by including three types of endurance exercise you alternate the use of different muscle groups, reducing the risk of overuse injuries. The benefits to your cardiovascular system are similar for each aerobic activity as long as you follow the basic principles of endurance exercise explained later in this chapter.

Fartlek Training

Fartlek is a Swedish term that means speed play. Fartlek training represents an exercise program with periods of faster-paced activity interspersed with periods of slower-paced activity. However, unlike interval training, fartlek exercise is more impulsive, or playful, in nature. Whenever you feel like picking up the pace you do so, for as long as you desire. For example, you may row at a moderate pace for a few minutes, then row very fast for several seconds, then row easily for a couple of minutes before again rowing at a powerful pace. You do not time the various segments of your training session but simply exercise as you feel throughout your entire workout, without any attempt at regimentation.

Cardiovascular Training Design

Although endurance exercise can provide many physical benefits, you must train in a certain manner to maximize cardiovascular conditioning. Because the effectiveness of endurance exercise methods varies considerably, we recommend the same training principles researched by the American College of Sports Medicine.[6] These highly respected exercise guidelines provide a solid framework for improving your endurance fitness safely and productively. For maximum cardiovascular benefit, we suggest that you do a variety of aerobic activities that use large muscle groups, can be maintained continuously, and are rhythmic in nature.

Exercise Selection and Order

Many aerobic activities meet the criteria of continuous large muscle exercise.[6] They include walking, jogging, running, cycling, cross-country skiing, aerobic dancing, rope skipping, rowing, stepping, swimming, in-line skating, and endurance sports such as soccer and basketball.

Most people do one endurance activity at a time, such as a 5-mile run or a 15-mile bicycle ride. Because of the high rate of overuse injuries, however, single-exercise endurance training is not recommended. Cross-training with two or more aerobic activities is a better alternative because it provides more comprehensive conditioning, has a lower risk of overuse injuries, and is more interesting. Common cross-training exercises include cycling, running, stepping, and rowing, as well as other combinations of endurance activities that complement each other.

Don't worry about a specific order for performing cross-training activities. Except for triathletes, who must swim first, cycle second, and run third, the exercise order is a matter of personal preference. Each aerobic activity produces about the same benefits for your cardiovascular system but uses different muscle groups. For example, swimming emphasizes the upper body, cycling works the leg muscles, and rowing targets both the upper and lower body muscle groups.

Although outdoor activities such as walking and bicycling are attractive options, these may not be the best choices for everyone. Safe outdoor walking or cycling requires sidewalks, bike paths, or roads with little traffic to avoid accidents. Weather and surface conditions, such as rain, snow, or ice, can interfere with your outdoor exercise program. For a variety of control factors, beginners who are overweight or otherwise out of shape usually find well-designed endurance equipment more appropriate. Such equipment provides structural stability and training consistency, with precise exercise conditions that you can repeat or change progressively each workout.

If you are unfit, recumbent cycling is the best activity to initiate your endurance training program (see figure 6.3). First, the recumbent cycle supports the back and body weight, eliminating weight-bearing forces that could overstress weak muscles and joints. Second, the recumbent cycle places the body in a more horizontal position, improving blood circulation and cardiovascular function. Third, the recumbent cycle provides electronic resistance that you can adjust to any fitness level, rather than body weight resistance, which may be too much for your present level of physical conditioning.

From here you can progress to upright cycling, which is similar to recumbent cycling except for the body position (see figure 6.4). Upright cycling requires greater postural control and a little more cardiovascular effort. It also provides electronic resistance that can be precisely and progressively increased as your fitness level improves.

The next recommended activity is treadmill walking (see figure 6.5). This is the most natural and least stressful weight-bearing exercise. Because walking is mostly a horizontal movement, it is not too demanding on your muscular or cardiovascular system. Of course, you may raise the treadmill incline, walk faster, or progress to jogging as your aerobic condition improves.

Stepping (see figure 6.6) is more demanding than cycling and walking because its vertical movement pattern lifts the body directly against the force of gravity with every step you take. You should develop at least a moderate level of cardiovascular conditioning before you add stepping to your exercise program.

Perhaps the most comprehensive and challenging piece of endurance equipment is the rowing machine (see figure 6.7). Rowing requires sequential activation of the leg, lower back, upper back, and arm muscles in a coordinated and controlled movement pattern. Although your body weight is supported, rowing is a more advanced form of aerobic activity that is better suited to well-conditioned individuals.

■ **Figure 6.3**   Recumbent cycle.   ■ **Figure 6.4**   Upright cycle.

■ **Figure 6.5** Treadmill.　　　　　　　　■ **Figure 6.6** Stepping machine.

■ **Figure 6.7** Rowing machine.

Of course, you may perform the activity you choose at various effort levels. For example, you may do a low-effort walk on a flat treadmill or a high-effort run on an inclined treadmill. Naturally, you can train longer at a slower pace than you can at a faster pace. Just remember the key to achieving cardiovascular fitness is following the basic endurance training principles, always using the large muscle groups in continuous and rhythmic movement patterns.

Exercise Frequency

Although endurance exercise affects your muscular system, its primary purpose is cardiovascular conditioning. You should perform at least two aerobic workouts a week to improve your cardiovascular fitness.[6] More is not necessarily better—three sessions a week produces almost the same results as five workouts. This is encouraging news for busy people! In fact, training more than three to five days a week increases the risk of injury without adding cardiovascular benefits.[19]

For most people, three days of endurance training a week are adequate. If you choose to train more frequently, however, try to limit very challenging workouts to three sessions a week.

Exercise Duration

Short bursts of exercise can enhance muscular strength, but longer workouts of continuous activity are necessary to improve cardiovascular endurance. For example, each set of strength exercise requires about 1 minute, but a session of endurance activity may take 20 to 60 minutes.

Strength training is high-intensity, low-duration exercise, whereas endurance training is low-intensity, high-duration exercise. Within certain limits, endurance exercise may also vary considerably in intensity and duration. For example, 30 minutes of running and 60 minutes of walking are different aerobic activities that require approximately the same amount of energy.[20] When the total work you do is about equal, shorter sessions of faster-paced endurance exercise and longer sessions of slower-paced endurance exercise will give you similar improvements in cardiovascular fitness.

Generally speaking, you should begin with slower-paced aerobic activities that are well within your fitness ability and place less stress on your body. Start with just a few minutes of endurance exercise and gradually increase the activity duration. At some point in your training progression, the exercise pace may seem too easy and the exercise duration may seem too long. When this happens, gradually increase the exercise pace and decrease the exercise duration until your training session is more satisfying. Soon you'll be covering the same "ground" in much less time.

Although your workout duration is largely a matter of personal preference, it is important to stay within the range of 20 to 60 minutes.[6] Doing less than 20 minutes of aerobic activity may decrease the benefits of your training, while completing more than 60 minutes of endurance exercise may increase your risk of overuse injury.

People who perform 20 to 30 minutes of aerobic activity are more likely to stay with their training programs than those who attempt 50 to 60 minutes. In our time-pressured society, long training sessions seem more difficult to maintain on a regular basis. Many people find that 20 to 30 minutes of strength training combined with 20 to 30 minutes of endurance training creates a practical and productive program for improving overall physical fitness.

Exercise Intensity

Exercise intensity is the effort level at which you perform aerobic activity. A simple means of rating your exercise intensity is referred to as the "talk test." If you can talk normally, your effort is most likely low. If you are able to speak only in short sentences, your effort is most likely moderate. But if you are not capable of carrying on a conversation at all, your level of effort is definitely high.

Although the talk test provides a reasonable estimate of your training intensity, it is clearly subjective in nature. For example, some people may rate a moderate effort as light, while others may consider a moderate effort to be heavy. For this reason, you should use a more objective method of determining your exercise effort, at least until you become familiar with these rating relationships.

Because heart rate is closely related to training effort, heart rate monitoring is a more precise means of assessing your exercise intensity. Generally speaking, your maximum heart rate can be estimated by subtracting your age from 220. For example, if you are 40 years old, your predicted maximum heart rate is about 180 beats per minute. If you are 50 years old, your predicted maximum heart rate is about 170 beats per minute. As you can see, your maximum heart rate decreases by approximately one beat per year throughout adult life. This is a normal part of the aging process and does not limit your ability to achieve a high level of aerobic fitness. Table 6.2 lists predicted maximum heart rates for men and women between 20 and 90 years of age.

Your maximum heart rate corresponds to an all-out exercise effort in which you are pumping as much oxygen-rich blood as possible to the working muscles. Of course, you can only train at maximum physical capacity for a short time, and such intense exercise is not appropriate for cardiovascular conditioning. Generally, you should train at about 70 percent of your maximum heart rate, although beginning exercisers should start at around 60 percent. If you are extremely fit, exercise at about 80 percent of your maximum heart rate. Check table 6.2 to determine your appropriate exercise heart rate. Of course, you will have to monitor your heart rate periodically during your training session to make sure you are within your target training zone.

Table 6.2   Predicted Maximum Age-Related Heart Rates and Selected Percentages for Training

Age	60%	70%	80%	100%
20	120	140	160	200
25	117	136	156	195
30	114	133	152	190
35	111	129	148	185
40	108	126	144	180
45	105	122	140	175
50	102	119	136	170
55	99	115	132	165
60	96	112	128	160
65	93	108	124	155
70	90	105	120	150
75	87	101	116	145
80	84	98	112	140
85	81	94	108	135
90	78	91	104	130

Figure 6.8 Count your pulse for 10 seconds then resume exercising.

Because it is difficult to feel your pulse when you are exercising, simply pause for 10 seconds every 10 minutes during a workout. Place your fingers on your wrist and keep your eyes on the clock as you count every heartbeat for 10 seconds (figure 6.8). Multiply by six to determine your training heart rate in beats per minute. For example, if you count 20 beats in 10 seconds, your exercise heart rate is about 120 beats per minute. If you take your pulse for more than 10 seconds, your heart rate may slow down so much that you will underestimate your actual training heart rate.

As you gain experience monitoring your exercise heart rate, you will correlate heart rate response with talking ability. That is, you can closely estimate your exercise heart rate based on your subjective assessment of the training effort. Nonetheless, you should periodically check your pulse during exercise because factors other than activity level may affect your heart rate. For example, high heat or humidity, psychological stress, and physical illness make the heart work harder than usual at a given exercise pace.

As you become more fit, you may increase your exercise intensity and train at higher effort levels. Just be sure to avoid overtraining and risking overuse injuries. Unless you are a competitive endurance athlete, you need not exercise harder than 80 percent of your maximum heart rate because you do not gain additional cardiovascular fitness benefits by training at higher heart rate levels. After you surpass the beginning exercise level, you should train between 70 to 80 percent of your maximum heart rate for most practical purposes.

Summary

Although you should not overdo endurance exercise, appropriate amounts of aerobic activity provide many physiological benefits. Regular endurance exercise improves physical function, aerobic capacity, and cardiovascular health. Because the heart serves as the fuel pump for the body, a well-conditioned cardiovascular system enables your muscles to work better and longer, with less effort and faster recovery.

Remember the general principles of endurance exercise when you select workout activities or determine training frequency, duration, and intensity. To best condition the cardiovascular system, be sure to choose aerobic activities that use large muscle groups, can be maintained continuously, and are rhythmic in nature. Cycling, walking, jogging, stepping, and rowing are all appropriate activities. Just be sure to introduce them in order of their physical demands. Train up to an hour, three to five days a week, although 20- to 30-minute segments are the practical approach for most people. Generally, endurance exercise should require a moderate level of physical effort.

Endurance Training Equipment and Exercises

Proper performance of endurance exercise involves more than just getting on a piece of aerobic equipment and working out as hard as you can for as long as you can. As with strength training, you should understand certain techniques and be familiar with each machine's features before beginning your exercise program.

The fitness industry offers many types of endurance exercise equipment, and within each category, many variations in design, function, and performance exist. In this chapter, four popular endurance training machines (upright and recumbent cycles, treadmills, steppers, and rowers) and procedures for using them will be discussed. But first we present some general guidelines for endurance training.

General Training Guidelines

No single method of using an exercise cycle, treadmill, stepper, or rowing machine exists. But it's important to follow general guidelines for safe and productive training.

Regardless of the activity you choose, be sure to check with your personal physician before beginning cardiovascular exercise. You may also want to consult with a professional exercise instructor if you train at a fitness facility or with a certified personal trainer if you work out at home.

If you dress appropriately for exercise, you will enhance your performance and reduce the risk of injury. Proper footwear is first and foremost, especially for weight-bearing activities such as walking, jogging, and stepping. You should wear supportive, well-cushioned athletic shoes that fit loosely around your toes and snugly around your heels.

Because exercise produces heat, your clothing should allow heat transfer from the body to the environment. Ordinarily, you should wear light athletic clothing, such as a T-shirt and shorts. But if you tend to feel cool in the first few minutes of exercise, wear an athletic suit or sweatshirt that you can easily remove as you warm up and begin to perspire. Be careful not to overdress because this prevents perspiration from evaporating; when you are exercising vigorously, evaporation of perspiration from the skin is essential for releasing body heat.

Along this same line, it is important to stay well hydrated throughout the exercise session. Drink plenty of fluids—preferably water—before each workout. To replace water while exercising, drink often from a water bottle at your activity station. Because you probably will lose more water than you can consume during exercise, be sure to continue drinking after your workout. You may substitute fruit juices and sport drinks for water, but avoid caffeinated or alcoholic beverages because they have a dehydrating effect. As a rule, you should drink at least eight glasses of water each day.

Be sure to begin each endurance training session with a progressive warm-up, work at a moderate effort level, train for a reasonable duration, stay within your target heart rate zone, and end with a gradual cool-down. Most important, train on a regular basis three or more days a week, unless you are ill or injured.

Monitoring your training progress is an excellent motivator, so record each exercise session in a training logbook. Keep track of your exercise activity, intensity level, training duration, exercise heart rate, and other pertinent information. Review your logbook whenever you need an extra boost of exercise enthusiasm. When you see how much you have improved, you'll realize how much your training investment has paid off. The logbook also provides valuable information to guide you as you plan progressively more difficult workouts.

Endurance Training Machines and Procedures

Now you're ready to learn specific training procedures for using endurance exercise equipment. Let's begin with a less stressful form of aerobic activity—upright and recumbent cycling.

Upright and Recumbent Cycles

The most obvious difference between the more traditional upright cycle and the more recent recumbent cycle is body position. Upright cycles require a vertical posture; in contrast, recumbent cycles require a more horizontal exercise position. One advantage of the recumbent cycle is back and neck support. Another benefit of the horizontal position is enhanced blood flow from the legs back to the heart. At the same effort level, your heart rate stays slightly lower during recumbent cycling than during upright cycling.[1] Both recumbent and upright cycling stress the quadriceps and the hamstrings by placing fairly equal emphasis on knee extension and hip extension. Upright cycles with moving handles add an upper body aspect to each exercise session.

Well-designed exercise cycles offer a wide range of exercise levels to accommodate various fitness abilities. They also provide several exercise programs to choose from, ranging from steady pace training to interval training. Whatever you select, don't forget that each exercise program should begin with a progressive warm-up and finish with a gradual cool-down.

The following steps should be followed when using upright or recumbent cycles:

1. Adjust the seat so that your knees are slightly bent when your feet are in the extended pedal positions (see figure 7.1, a and b). Slide each foot as far into the pedal strap as is comfortable, with the ball of the foot over the pedal pivot point. Make sure your hips are fully supported by the seat. If using a recumbent cycle, place your hands across your lap or on the sides of the seat, and rest your back comfortably against the seat back.

2. Turn on the exercise monitor and select an appropriate exercise profile. Choose a program with a progressive warm-up, a gradual cool-down, and a constant training level in between.

3. Adjust the effort level to your current fitness ability. Level 1, 2, or 3 is recommended for beginners; level 4, 5, or 6 for intermediate exercisers; and level 7, 8, or 9 for advanced participants.

4. Adjust the exercise time according to your fitness level. If you're a beginner, stay in the range of 2 to 10 minutes. If you consider yourself moderately fit, exercise for 10 to 20 minutes. If you're in pretty good shape, train for 20 to 30 minutes. Competitive athletes may wish to exercise longer, but if your primary purpose is cardiovascular fitness, you don't need to cycle more than 30 minutes.

5. Keep your pedaling speed approximately 20 miles per hour, or about 80 pedal revolutions per minute. If the bike has a pacer, do your best to stay with the pacer throughout the exercise program.

After completing the course, be sure to cool down with a slower but still continuous pedaling action, then walk around to finish the cool-down.

A

B

■ **Figure 7.1** *(a)* Proper positioning on a recumbent cycle. *(b)* Proper positioning on an upright cycle.

Motor-Driven Treadmills

There are two basic types of treadmills—those that are self-propelled and those that are motor-driven. Although considerably more expensive, motor-driven treadmills are clearly superior in design, function, and durability. Good motor-driven treadmills have enough horsepower to maintain the desired speed and to keep the track from slipping. The track should be strong and stable to maximize exercise performance yet cushioned and resilient to minimize stress on the feet, legs, and lower back. Sturdy handrails and convenient switches are a must for training safety.

The two major program variables in treadmill training are speed and inclination. Well-designed treadmills provide walking and running speeds between 2 and 10 miles per hour. This accommodates the individual who walks at a 30-minute-mile pace as well as the person who runs at a 6-minute-mile pace.

The greater the treadmill inclination, the greater the exercise effort at a given training speed. For example, if you prefer not to run, you can make your walking workout more challenging by increasing the treadmill inclination. For most practical purposes, treadmills should incline up to 7 degrees.

Treadmill walking and running should begin and end with slower-paced warm-up and cool-down segments. The actual conditioning session may consist of steady pace activity or interval exercise, depending on how you change the treadmill speed and inclination.

Before you begin, note where the handlebars and stop switch are located in case you lose your balance. Follow these guidelines when using a motorized treadmill:

1. Straddle the track with your feet on the solid side frames, place one hand on the handlebar, and touch the power switch with the other hand. Push the "grade down" button to make sure the treadmill is at zero degrees and completely level. If the treadmill offers preprogrammed exercise protocols, select the desired workout.

2. Touch the start switch and the track should begin moving slowly. While holding the handrail, place one foot gently on the track and stride with one leg to feel the movement speed. When comfortable, place both feet on the moving track and walk naturally while still holding the handrail.

3. When you feel confident, let go of the handrail, first with one hand and then the other, and walk naturally. Be sure to stay on the front portion of the track, to keep you close to the handrail and controls and to reduce the risk of drifting off the back of the track. Your exercise posture greatly influences your treadmill performance. Try to walk or run "tall," with normal stride length and natural arm action (see figure 7.2). Avoid short, choppy steps and allow your arms to move smoothly in coordination with your legs. That is, your right arm and left leg should move forward and backward together, and your left arm and right leg should move together. Focus your eyes forward rather than downward. Keep your shoulders and hips square without allowing your torso to swing side to side or to shift forward or backward.

4. At this point you will probably want to walk faster, so touch the speed button to quicken your pace. Be sure to increase the miles per hour gradually as you progress to your desired training speed. Once you reach 4 miles per hour, you are walking at a relatively fast 15-minute-mile pace. To further increase your effort, raise the grade slightly so that you are walking uphill. For every treadmill training session, you should warm up and cool down for a few minutes at a slow speed and low grade. For the actual training phase, choose a moderate effort level, selecting a track speed and elevation that raises your heart rate to about 70 percent of maximum.

5. If you are in poor condition, try a training duration of 2 to 10 minutes; if you are moderately fit, do 10 to 20 minutes; and if you are very fit, work out for 20 to 30 minutes.

6. As you prepare to finish your exercise session, gradually reduce the speed and grade to the lowest levels, grasp the handrail, and touch the stop switch. Do not dismount the track until it has stopped moving completely.

If at any time you feel uncomfortable, off balance, or out of control, immediately touch the stop switch and the track will gently but quickly stop. As an alternative to a steady pace program, you may perform a variety of interval training workouts. For example, you could do three minutes at a slower than normal pace, followed by three minutes at a faster than normal pace, alternated throughout the exercise session. Whatever training program you use, be sure to advance the controls one unit at a time since the track speed and elevation changes are electronically delayed.

■ **Figure 7.2** Proper positioning on a treadmill.

Steppers

Initially introduced as actual stair-climbing machines with revolving staircases, steppers have become popular endurance training tools. A vigorous exercise, stepping places high demands on the cardiovascular system.[2] It produced higher heart rate responses than cycling, treadmill walking, and jogging when these activities were performed at the same effort level (see table 7.1). This occurs because stepping requires lifting the body weight vertically, which uses more energy than most other endurance exercises. Research participants rated stepping higher than other aerobic activities for both muscular and cardiovascular effort, which may make it more appropriate for intermediate exercisers than for beginners (see table 7.2). You may select a steady pace step program or a more challenging interval training program.

Step machines fall into two general categories based on their movement mechanics. Independent steppers have separated foot pedals that work independently of each other; neither foot pedal influences the action of the other. Dependent steppers have connected foot pedals that work in coordination. In other words, as the left foot pedal moves upward, the right foot pedal moves downward and vice versa. Since the foot pedal arrangement has little effect on the cardiovascular benefits or energy requirements of stepping, the choice between independent or dependent step machines is largely a matter of personal preference.

Muscle involvement in stepping is closely related to your exercise technique. The quadriceps and hamstrings provide most of the movement force. The calf muscles of the lower leg are also involved, particularly if you perform much of the stepping action on your toes.

Table 7.1 Heart Rate and Blood Pressure Responses on Endurance Machines

Exercise time (minutes)	Cycle		Stepper		Treadmill		Skate machine	
	HR	BP	HR	BP	HR	BP	HR	BP
4	96	133/76	110	137/74	92	129/74	103	131/71
8	130	153/74	140	148/74	123	143/71	116	145/75
12	138	161/77	143	155/76	126	149/74	127	154/75
16	140	159/76	150	156/72	135	154/73	128	151/76
20	109	135/75	124	135/74	99	134/73	109	135/74
Mean	123	148/76	133	146/74	115	142/73	117	144/74

Test subjects were 42 years old, having a target heart rate range of 107 to 160 beats per minute.

Table 7.2 Rating of Exercise Factors on Endurance Machines

	Cycle	Stepper	Treadmill	Skate machine
Muscular effort	3.3	4.4	2.8	4.1
Cardiovascular effort	3.8	4.6	3.8	3.5
Coordination required	2.2	3.3	2.8	4.6
Overall fitness benefit	3.8	4.4	3.9	3.7
Exercise satisfaction	3.8	4.2	3.6	3.7

1 = low, 5 = high

You may inadvertently involve the muscles of your upper body if you do not use appropriate stepping posture. Proper stepping form requires a fairly upright posture, using the hands for balance rather than for body support (see figure 7.3). Avoid leaning forward and unnecessarily stressing your wrists and lower back, which is not the intent of stepping exercise. As with walking and running, strive to keep your head up and your back straight while stepping.

The depth of your steps should be moderate and comfortable. Just as there is no set stride length for walking and running, there is no set step depth for stepping. Shallow stepping may decrease muscular work, and deep stepping may increase the risk of injury. A moderate stepping action gives you a reasonable range of movement, effectively involving the leg muscles while still maintaining level hips and shoulders.

Because stepping is a demanding physical activity, it is essential to spend the first few minutes warming up and the last few minutes cooling down during each session. Your actual workout may consist of a steady stepping cadence or a series of high-effort and low-effort intervals. Just be sure to maintain proper form and to remain within your target heart rate zone at all times.

Use the following guidelines when using a step machine:

1. Step on the pedals and record your body weight according to the computer prompts.

2. Choose an exercise program that has built-in warm-up and cool-down phases with a constant training pace in between. If your present level of fitness is low, train at effort level 1, 2, or 3; if your present fitness level is moderate, train at effort level

4, 5, or 6; and if your present fitness level is high, try effort level 7, 8, or 9. As you exercise, you can make the workout harder or easier by adjusting the effort and pace controls.

3. Select an appropriate exercise duration. Beginners should start with 2 to 10 minutes of exercise, intermediate exercisers may train for 10 to 20 minutes, and advanced exercisers for 20 to 30 minutes.

4. Take medium steps and maintain level hips and shoulders.

5. After you finish your exercise session, dismount the stepper and walk for a few minutes to finish the cool-down.

Rowing Machines

Rowing machines come in various shapes, sizes, and resistance modes. Perhaps the most realistic rowers are those that use revolving paddles and air resistance, but hydraulic and electric models provide similar cardiovascular benefits.

Although people sometimes think of rowing as an upper body activity, it uses the legs and lower back as well as the upper back and

■ **Figure 7.3**   Proper positioning on a step machine.

arms. The first movement in the rowing stroke is simultaneous extension of the knees and hips, a leg-pushing action that uses the quadriceps, hamstrings, and gluteal muscles. This is followed by trunk extension produced by the erector spinae muscles in the lower back. The final action in the rowing stroke is the arm pull, accomplished primarily by the latissimus dorsi, rhomboids, and trapezius muscles of the upper back and the biceps muscles of the arms. All of the rowing movements should be performed smoothly and sequentially, with a firm but relaxed hand grip, an upright head, and a moderate range of trunk extension. Don't approach a horizontal torso position, as this can place excessive stress on your lower back. On the return movement, reverse the muscular actions to come forward quickly, gently, and easily in preparation for your next pull.

To facilitate these successive and coordinated body movements, well-designed rowing machines should be structurally stable and operationally smooth. There should be no sticking points or rough spots in the pulling movement, and the return action should be easy to perform.

The rowing action will vary according to your stroke, which is dependent on the length of your arms and legs as well as your training technique. Whatever your rowing cadence, the key to cardiovascular conditioning is your heart rate response to the exercise effort. Try to work within your training heart rate range, which means you should be able to talk in short sentences during your rowing workout.

Follow these steps when using a rowing machine:

1. Sit on the moving seat and secure your feet to the footpads.

2. Grip the handle comfortably, with your knees, hips, and trunk flexed.

3. Push your body backward by extending your knees, hips, and trunk, and pull the handle to your midsection (see figure 7.4).

4. Return to the starting position as smoothly as possible.

5. Begin with easy strokes until you are warmed up, then progressively increase your exercise effort.

6. Pulling harder or faster increases the exercise resistance and training intensity.

7. Finish your rowing workout with a few minutes of lower-effort strokes to cool down gradually.

8. Beginning rowers should strive for 2 to 10 minutes of continuous exercise, intermediate rowers should train for 10 to 20 minutes, and advanced rowers may complete 20 to 30 minutes of this activity.

Equipment Selection

The most important consideration when choosing endurance exercise equipment is personal preference. If you are a lively individual, then you may enjoy the unencumbered feeling of running on a treadmill. If you are overweight or otherwise out of shape, the supportive structure of a recumbent or upright cycle may make more sense as your basic training mode.

Of course, equipment availability may play a major role in your choice of aerobic activity. If you have access to cycles, treadmills, steppers, and rowers, then a cross-training program may make your workouts more enjoyable. By performing a combination of endurance exercises each workout or by changing aerobic activities every training session, you may increase both personal motivation and physical conditioning.

■ **Figure 7.4** Proper positioning on a rowing machine.

Choose the modes of endurance exercise that you like best. If you prefer a lower-intensity training experience, recumbent or upright cycling may be best for the majority of your endurance workouts. If you like more rhythmic forms of aerobic activity, the rowing machine may be the perfect piece of exercise equipment. If you are already in moderately good shape and want a high-intensity workout that provides the most training benefit in the least amount of time, try stepping. And if you prefer an activity that combines both rhythm and intensity, treadmill walking and running are good choices.

Summary

Approach endurance exericse sensibly. A "no gain without pain" attitude may do more harm than good. Before beginning your training program, familiarize yourself with the guidelines at the beginning of this chapter.

You have many choices of endurance exercise, and each of these endurance activities effectively conditions the cardiovascular system. Therefore, your choice of exercise equipment is largely a matter of personal preference and physical condition.

Well-designed aerobic exercise equipment is scientifically sound, permits gradual warming up and cooling down, provides a variety of training levels and programs, displays performance feedback, offers user-friendly operation, and keeps the risk of injury to a minimum. Always use an exercise machine as directed in the manufacturer's handbook, and always apply the endurance training principles.

Circuit Training

Circuit training typically involves a series of different exercises that you perform sequentially and continuously for one or more rounds. That is, you select several specific exercises and move quickly from station to station to maximize both training effectiveness and time-efficiency. For example, you could complete one circuit of 15 strength exercises in about 20 minutes (1 minute for each exercise with 20 seconds between exercise stations). As another example, you could perform two circuits of 4 endurance exercises in about 26 minutes (3 minutes for each exercise with 20 seconds between exercise stations).

Perhaps the most challenging and comprehensive circuit training program is one that combines both strength and endurance exercise. This is generally accomplished by alternating strength and endurance stations throughout the circuit. For example, you could complete an alternating circuit of 10 strength exercises and 10 endurance exercises in about 20 minutes if you allow 40 seconds for each exercise with 20 seconds between exercise stations.

Of course, you can set up the circuit training protocol any way you choose. However, there are certain basic principles that apply to the three standard circuit training programs. Let's take a look at the general guidelines for designing strength circuits, strength and endurance circuits, and endurance circuits.

Circuit Strength Training

Muscular strength is developed through high-effort anaerobic activity, which fatigues the target muscle groups within 90 seconds of resistance exercise. In the past, people typically performed three sets of each strength exercise, resting two to three minutes between successive sets for sufficient muscle recovery. Of course, this resulted in relatively long training sessions, with much more time spent resting than exercising.

To reduce the workout duration, with a minimum percentage of resting time and a maximum percentage of activity time, circuit training involves one set of an exercise followed as quickly as possible by one set of another exercise for a different muscle group. For example, you could not do two 10-repetition sets of the leg extension exercise with the same weight load without resting between sets.

However, you could do a 10-repetition set of leg extensions followed immediately by a 10-repetition set of leg curls because each exercise addresses different muscle groups.

People who prefer to complete more than one set of each exercise can simply go through the circuit two or three times. By so doing, they accomplish the same training volume as traditional multiple-set training but in much less time because they essentially eliminate the rest periods between sets.

Research on circuit strength training has produced remarkable results, even when the participants performed only one set of each exercise. And the results are not limited to increased muscular strength. Although each resistance exercise is completed within the anaerobic energy system, the continuous and high-effort muscular activity maintains at least a moderate cardiovascular response throughout the entire training session.

For example, research completed at Wake Forest University showed a 10 percent increase in cardiovascular fitness after 10 weeks of circuit strength training, as much as a second group who did 10 weeks of running.[1] The participants also gained as much strength as a third group that did 10 weeks of standard free weight training. The circuit workout consisted of 12 Nautilus exercises; the subjects performed one set of each exercise with as little recovery time as possible between stations. When coupled with endurance exercise, even greater improvements in cardiovascular fitness can be achieved.[2]

One approach to setting up the strength exercises in a circuit training program is to simply alternate opposing muscle groups, starting with the larger leg muscles and finishing with the smaller midsection muscles. A standard strength training circuit could be designed as presented in table 8.1.

Another design for a standard strength training circuit is to alternate lower body, upper body, and midsection exercises. Table 8.2 presents an example of this exercise arrangement.

Table 8.1 Sample Circuit Strength Training Program Alternating Opposing Muscles From Larger to Smaller Groups

Station	Exercise	Target muscles
1	Leg extension	Quadriceps
2	Leg curl	Hamstrings
3	Hip adduction	Hip adductors
4	Hip abduction	Hip abductors
5	Leg press	Quadriceps, hamstrings, gluteals
6	Chest cross	Pectoralis major
7	Pullover	Latissimus dorsi
8	Lateral raise	Deltoids
9	Biceps curl	Biceps
10	Triceps extension	Triceps
11	Low back	Erector spinae
12	Abdominal	Rectus abdominis

Note: The time allotted for each exercise is 60 seconds. The total time for one circuit is approximately 12 to 14 minutes.

Table 8.2   Sample Circuit Strength Training Program Alternating Lower Body, Upper Body, and Midsection Muscle Groups

Station	Exercise	Target muscles
1	Leg extension	Quadriceps
2	Chest cross	Pectoralis major
3	Leg curl	Hamstrings
4	Pullover	Latissimus dorsi
5	Hip adduction	Hip adductors
6	Lateral raise	Deltoids
7	Hip abduction	Hip abductors
8	Biceps curl	Biceps
9	Leg press	Quadriceps, hamstrings, gluteals
10	Triceps extension	Triceps
11	Low back	Erector spinae
12	Abdominal	Rectus abdominis

Note: The time allotted for each exercise is 60 seconds. The total time for one circuit is approximately 12 to 14 minutes.

Generally speaking, each exercise in a standard strength training circuit is performed for one set of 8 to 12 controlled repetitions. Typically, one minute is allotted to complete each set and 20 seconds are allotted to move between exercise stations. Depending on the program objectives, participants may complete one, two, or three rounds of the circuit. More rounds of the circuit require more energy and place greater emphasis on endurance conditioning. In a single circuit, the exercise resistance may be 65 to 75 percent of maximum. However, when performing multiple circuits, the exercise resistance must be reduced accordingly (55 to 65 percent of maximum).

Circuit Strength and Endurance Training

As indicated in the previous section, a combined circuit training program of strength and endurance exercise can offer a comprehensive conditioning experience. Combined circuit training programs can take many forms, but the typical protocol alternates strength and endurance exercises, with 30 to 40 seconds of activity at each exercise station. Because of the cumulative effects of combined strength and endurance exercise, the shorter exercise bouts are productive for improving both muscular and cardiovascular fitness.[2] In fact, longer intervals in a combined circuit training program would be too demanding for all but the most fit exercisers. There is essentially no rest between the alternating strength and endurance segments, so the combined circuit training protocol places high demands on both the anaerobic and aerobic energy systems. And although it is not as effective for muscle development as a basic strength circuit nor as effective for cardiovascular development as a basic endurance circuit, combined circuit training may be the most efficient method for overall physical conditioning purposes.

A recommended combined circuit training program intersperses the strength exercises presented in table 8.2 with running in place or stationary cycling. Each strength exercise and each endurance exercise is performed continuously for 30 seconds. The strength exercises should be reduced in both resistance and repetitions for consistency in completing the circuit. As a rule, you should perform 6 to 10 repetitions of each strength exercise, using about 45 to 55 percent of your maximum resistance. A sample combined circuit training protocol is described in table 8.3.

Table 8.3 Sample Circuit Strength and Endurance Training Program Alternating Strength and Endurance Exercises

Station	Exercise	Target muscles
1	Leg extension	Quadriceps
2	Jogging	Heart, hamstrings
3	Chest cross	Pectoralis major
4	Cycling	Heart, quadriceps
5	Leg curl	Hamstrings
6	Jogging	Heart, hamstrings
7	Pullover	Latissimus dorsi
8	Cycling	Heart, quadriceps
9	Hip adduction	Hip adductors
10	Jogging	Heart, hamstrings
11	Lateral raise	Deltoids
12	Cycling	Heart, quadriceps
13	Hip abduction	Hip abductors
14	Jogging	Heart, hamstrings
15	Biceps curl	Biceps
16	Cycling	Heart, quadriceps
17	Leg press	Quadriceps, hamstrings, gluteals
18	Jogging	Heart, hamstrings
19	Triceps extension	Triceps
20	Cycling	Heart, quadriceps
21	Low back	Erector spinae
22	Jogging	Heart, hamstrings
23	Abdominal	Rectus abdominis
24	Cycling	Heart, quadriceps

Note: The time allotted for each exercise is 30 seconds. The total time for one circuit is approximately 12 to 15 minutes.

Circuit Endurance Training

Although not as popular as circuit strength training, circuit endurance training is a most interesting and effective means of improving cardiovascular fitness. One advantage of circuit endurance training over continuous endurance exercise (e.g., jogging, cycling, or stepping) is the frequent change in exercise mode. In addition to preventing boredom, changing activities every few minutes emphasizes different muscle groups for more intense exercise experiences.

For example, you may begin with stationary cycling (which emphasizes the quadriceps muscles), then do treadmill walking (which primarily works the hamstring muscles), followed by stair stepping (which places more stress on the quadriceps and calf muscles). The circuit can be finished with rowing, which provides more balanced training for the lower-body pushing muscles (quadriceps and hamstrings) and the upper-body pulling muscles (erector spinae, latissimus dorsi, trapezius, rhomboids, and biceps).

To reach what is known as a steady state of cardiovascular response, spending 3 to 5 minutes at each circuit station is recommended. As presented in table 8.4, you could do 3 minutes each of four endurance exercises and go around the circuit three times. This would give you almost 40 minutes of continuous but varied aerobic activity (4 exercises × 3 minutes each × 3 circuits = 36 minutes plus 20-second transition periods between the endurance equipment stations).

Table 8.4   Sample Circuit Endurance Training Program Alternating Exercises With Different Muscle Emphasis

Station	Exercise	Target muscles
1	Stationary cycling	Heart, quadriceps
2	Treadmill walking	Heart, hamstrings
3	Stair stepping	Heart, quadriceps, calves
4	Rowing	Heart, quadriceps, hamstrings, erector spinae, latissimus dorsi, trapezius, rhomboids, biceps

Note: The time allotted for each exercise is 3 minutes. The total time for one circuit is approximately 12 to 13 minutes.

Of course, you can design an endurance training circuit in many ways. For example, if you perform 5 minutes at each station, one trip around the circuit would provide about a 20-minute cardiovascular workout (4 exercises × 5 minutes each × 1 circuit = 20 minutes). On the other hand, you could experience a moderate-length circuit endurance training session (about 30 minutes) by doing 4 minutes at each station and completing two circuits (4 exercises × 4 minutes each × 2 circuits = 32 minutes).

Although circuit endurance training does not reduce the total workout time, it provides a more interesting means of attaining aerobic activity benefits. In fact, because you frequently change the exercise mode (every 3 to 5 minutes), you can typically train harder than when you perform a single activity for a prolonged period of time (20 to 30 minutes). The variety of exercises also reduces the risk of overuse injuries, making circuit endurance training both a safe and effective method for cardiovascular conditioning.

Summary

Circuit training is a continuous workout that consists of several different exercises performed successively with as little transition time as necessary between stations. Circuit strength training typically involves about 12 resistance exercises for different muscle groups, each of which is performed for one set of 8 to 12 repetitions.

Circuit strength and endurance training alternates strength exercises with stations for running or cycling. This is a more challenging workout that enhances both muscular strength and cardiovascular endurance with 30- to 40-second segments of each activity.

Circuit endurance training combines different aerobic exercises into a 20- to 40-minute session, with about 3 to 5 minutes of each activity. Alternating exercises that emphasize different muscle groups makes the workout more interesting and reduces the risk of overuse injuries.

Two-Month Training Programs

Now you're ready to put it all together and begin endurance and strength training. Beginners will want to start with the two-month training programs in this chapter. If you have already been training for some time and are ready for a greater challenge, skip ahead to the six-month training programs in chapter 10. If you're not certain where to begin, start with the programs in this chapter and advance when you feel sure you are ready.

Endurance Exercise

Start with less stressful endurance exercises with relatively low training intensity and duration. Spend two weeks on each type of exercise, systematically increasing your cardiovascular effort as indicated. Unless you have a strong preference otherwise, perform the endurance exercise before the strength exercise.

Strength Exercise

Now that you're familiar with the strength exercises, you need to know how to select and organize them into a systematic and successful training program. It's best to begin with a few basic strength training exercises, then gradually increase the number of exercises as your muscles become better conditioned. This establishes a solid base of support in the major muscle groups and permits progressive strength development. You should also do different strength exercises as your muscles become accustomed to your standard training routine. This prevents boredom and enhances the training effect.

Although your exercise facility may not have all of the equipment listed here, use this sample two-month training program as a guide for achieving better strength fitness, adapting the program to your needs and available equipment. This program is a highly effective and efficient means of muscular conditioning. Of course, you may repeat a week if you do not feel ready for the next training progression.

The sample two-month strength training program is presented with machine exercises. If you prefer free weight training, recommended exercises for the eight weeks of progressive strength training are presented at the end of this chapter.

Month One

This is your first month of serious and sensible strength exercise, so you must begin slowly to maximize positive muscle responses and prevent overdoing it. If you stay with the recommended exercise program, you should make excellent progress without experiencing any training setbacks. This month of training will be described week by week. Be sure to use the first and last 2 to 3 minutes of each session for warm-up and cool-down.

Month 1, Week 1

Begin with three basic strength exercises that address many key muscle areas: the leg press machine, the vertical chest machine, and the compound row machine (see program 9.1 on page 189). These three machines use 6 out of 12 major muscle groups.

Because all of these exercises are linear in nature, involving pushing or pulling in a straight line, they address more than one muscle group at the same time. By design, these exercises involve familiar movements that are important for daily activities and sport performance. The leg press strengthens both the quadriceps and hamstrings. The decline press strengthens the pectoralis major and triceps, and the compound row stresses the latissimus dorsi and biceps. You should do one set of 8 to 12 repetitions of each exercise. When you can do 12 repetitions, increase your training resistance by about 5 percent. Note the typical starting weight loads for these exercises based on your age and gender. Your actual starting weight loads must be determined by personal trial, beginning with light resistance and adding weight until you are in the 8- to 12-repetition range. If you cannot complete 8 repetitions, reduce the resistance to prevent overstressing your muscles and joints. To enhance endurance, perform 10 to 15 minutes of either upright or recumbent cycling at a low effort level.

Month 1, Week 2

During the second week of training, you may add two new exercises—the low back machine and the abdominal machine. Program 9.2 on page 190 lists the recommended exercise order and shows the major muscle groups these five exercises address.

The low back and abdominal exercises are rotary in nature (moving in an arc around a rotational axis) and, as indicated by their names, target the low back and abdominal muscles. Perform one set of 8 to 12 repetitions of each exercise. When you can do 12 repetitions, increase your training resistance by about 5 percent. Because low back problems and midsection weaknesses are common, begin these exercises with less than the standard starting weight loads. It is always better to begin too light and add resistance than to begin too heavy and risk injury. Continue cycling exercise for endurance enhancement. This week, try to complete 15 to 20 minutes of cycling at a low to moderate effort level.

Month 1, Week 3

Week three is a good time to add two new leg exercises—hip adduction and hip abduction. The recommended machine order and the major muscle groups addressed by this program are listed in program 9.3 on page 191.

The hip adduction exercise works the inner thigh muscles, and the hip abduction exercise targets the outer thigh muscles. Both are rotary exercises that strengthen the muscles responsible for lateral movement activities such as skating, skiing, tennis, and basketball.

Do one set of 8 to 12 repetitions of each exercise. When you can perform 12 repetitions, increase your training resistance by about 5 percent. Program 9.3 lists typical starting weight loads for these new leg exercises based on age and gender. This week, switch from cycling to treadmill walking. Begin with 15 to 20 minutes of moderate-effort walking on a flat track.

Month 1, Week 4

During the fourth week of training, you can add another upper body exercise as well as a machine that addresses the neck muscles. The recommended additions are the overhead press machine, a linear exercise that uses the deltoids and triceps, and the 4-way neck machine, typically used for the neck flexor and neck extensor muscles. Program 9.4 on page 192 lists the recommended exercise order and shows the major muscle groups addressed by these nine exercises. As you can see, you are now working all of the major muscle groups.

Do one set of 8 to 12 repetitions of each exercise. When you can reach 12 repetitions, increase your training resistance by about 5 percent. Typical starting weight loads for the overhead press exercise, the neck flexion exercise, and the neck extension exercise based on age and gender are listed in program 9.4. Increase your treadmill walking to 20 to 25 minutes of moderate effort, walking on a flat track or low incline.

Month Two

Congratulations on completing your first month of progressive strength and endurance training. During the second month of training, you may add several more exercises to round out your strength workouts. These exercises will provide a comprehensive program of muscle conditioning within relatively brief training sessions. This month of training will be described week by week.

Month 2, Week 1

As you begin your second month, add two strength exercises that target the upper arm muscles. The biceps curl machine provides rotary exercise for the biceps muscles, while the triceps extension machine provides rotary exercise for the triceps muscles. Both machines offer full-range strength training for their respective muscle groups. Program 9.5 on page 193 lists the recommended exercise order. These 11 machines address all of the major muscle groups with more direct training for the upper arm muscles.

Perform one set of 8 to 12 repetitions of each exercise. When you can complete 12 repetitions, increase your training resistance by about 5 percent. Program 9.5 shows typical starting weight loads for these new exercises based on age and gender. You should be ready for 15 to 20 minutes of stepping exercise performed at a moderate pace. Keep in mind that this activity may be more challenging than the cycling and walking.

Month 2, Week 2

This week you can add two specific exercises for the thigh muscles: the leg extension machine for the quadriceps and the leg curl machine for the hamstrings. Both machines provide rotary movement and full-range exercise for the largest muscle groups of the body (quadriceps and hamstrings). You will find the recommended exercise order and the major muscle involvement in program 9.6 on page 194.

Do one set of each exercise, beginning with a resistance that permits at least 8 repetitions, and increase the weight load by about 5 percent when you can complete 12 repetitions. The usual starting weight loads for the leg extension and leg curl machines are presented in program 9.6. Progress to 20 to 25 minutes of moderate-effort stepping, always paying attention to proper technique.

Month 2, Week 3

At this point in your training program, you may benefit from and enjoy performing two body weight exercises: chin-ups and bar dips on the weight-assisted chin/dip machine. The chin-up is a linear exercise that involves the latissimus dorsi and biceps muscles, whereas the bar dip is a linear exercise that works the pectoralis major and triceps muscles. The recommended exercise order and the muscle group utilization are presented in program 9.7 on page 195.

Complete one set of each exercise, starting with a counterbalance weight load that enables you to perform 8 repetitions. When you are capable of doing 12 repetitions, reduce the resistance by approximately 5 percent. Keep in mind that on the weight-assisted bar dip and chin-up exercises, decreasing the counterbalance weight load actually increases the training resistance (a larger percentage of your body weight). The typical beginning weight loads for weight-assisted chin-ups and bar dips are presented in program 9.7. After six weeks, you should be ready to try a rowing machine workout. Start with 15 to 20 minutes of moderate effort.

Month 2, Week 4

As you approach completion of your second training month, you can substitute more specific exercises for the pectoralis major, latissimus dorsi, and deltoid muscles. The pec dec machine can replace the vertical chest, the super pullover can replace the compound row, and the lateral raise can replace the overhead press. The new exercises better isolate the target torso muscles (pectoralis major, latissimus dorsi, deltoids) without involving the arm muscles (triceps, biceps). Program 9.8 on page 196 presents the recommended exercise order and the major muscle groups addressed in this program.

Perform one set of each exercise, using a resistance that enables you to perform 8 repetitions, and increase the weightload by 5 percent when you can complete 12 repetitions. Program 9.8 offers usual beginning weight loads for the pec dec, super pullover, and lateral raise exercises according to age and gender. Increase your rowing time to 20 to 25 minutes at a moderate effort level. You should feel more fluid as you master the sequential actions in this exercise.

Exercise order	Training sets	Training repetitions	Training speed[a]
1. Leg press	1	8-12	2/4
2. Vertical chest	1	8-12	2/4
3. Compound row	1	8-12	2/4

[a]Up and down in seconds.

Major muscle group	Machine
1. Quadriceps	Leg press
2. Hamstrings	Leg press
3. Hip adductors	–
4. Hip abductors	–
5. Pectoralis major	Vertical chest
6. Latissimus dorsi	Compound row
7. Deltoids	–
8. Biceps	Compound row
9. Triceps	Vertical chest
10. Low back	–
11. Abdominals	–
12. Neck	–

Age group	Leg press[a]	Vertical chest[a]	Compound row[a]
20-29			
Males	150.0	65.0	85.0
Females	100.0	40.0	55.0
30-39			
Males	137.5	60.0	80.0
Females	92.5	37.5	52.5
40-49			
Males	125.0	55.0	75.0
Females	85.0	35.0	50.0
50-59			
Males	112.5	50.0	70.0
Females	77.5	32.5	47.5
60-69			
Males	100.0	45.0	65.0
Females	70.0	30.0	45.0
70-79			
Males	87 s.5	40.0	60.0
Females	62.5	27.5	42.5

[a]Weight load in pounds.

Exercise order	Training sets	Training repetitions	Training speed[a]
1. Leg press	1	8-12	2/4
2. Vertical chest	1	8-12	2/4
3. Compound row	1	8-12	2/4
4. Low back[b]	1	8-12	2/4
5. Abdominal[b]	1	8-12	2/4

[a]Up and down in seconds.

[b]New exercises this week.

Major muscle group	Machine
1. Quadriceps	Leg press
2. Hamstrings	Leg press
3. Hip adductors	—
4. Hip abductors	—
5. Pectoralis major	Vertical chest
6. Latissimus dorsi	Compound row
7. Deltoids	—
8. Biceps	Compound row
9. Triceps	Vertical chest
10. Low back	Low back
11. Abdominals	Abdominal
12. Neck	—

Age group	Low back[a]	Abdominal[a]
20-29		
Males	70.0	70.0
Females	50.0	45.0
30-39		
Males	65.0	65.0
Females	47.5	42.5
40-49		
Males	60.0	60.0
Females	45.0	40.0
50-59		
Males	55.0	55.0
Females	42.5	37.5
60-69		
Males	50.0	50.0
Females	40.0	35.0
70-79		
Males	45.0	45.0
Females	37.5	32.5

[a]Weight load in pounds.

Exercise order	Training sets	Training repetitions	Training speed[a]
1. Leg press	1	8-12	2/4
2. Hip adductor[b]	1	8-12	2/4
3. Hip abductor[b]	1	8-12	2/4
4. Vertical chest	1	8-12	2/4
5. Compound row	1	8-12	2/4
6. Low back	1	8-12	2/4
7. Abdominal	1	8-12	2/4

[a]Up and down in seconds.

[b]New exercises this week.

Major muscle group	Machine
1. Quadriceps	Leg press
2. Hamstrings	Leg press
3. Hip adductors	Hip adductor
4. Hip abductors	Hip abductor
5. Pectoralis major	Vertical chest
6. Latissimus dorsi	Compound row
7. Deltoids	–
8. Biceps	Compound row
9. Triceps	Vertical chest
10. Low back	Low back
11. Abdominals	Abdominal
12. Neck	–

Age group	Hip abductor[a]	Hip adductor[a]
20-29		
Males	70.0	80.0
Females	45.0	55.0
30-39		
Males	65.0	75.0
Females	42.5	52.5
40-49		
Males	60.0	70.0
Females	40.0	50.0
50-59		
Males	55.0	65.0
Females	37.5	47.5
60-69		
Males	50.0	60.0
Females	35.0	45.0
70-79		
Males	45.0	55.0
Females	32.5	42.5

[a]Weight load in pounds.

Exercise order	Training sets	Training repetitions	Training speed[a]
1. Leg press	1	8-12	2/4
2. Hip adductor	1	8-12	2/4
3. Hip abductor	1	8-12	2/4
4. Vertical chest	1	8-12	2/4
5. Compound row	1	8-12	2/4
6. Overhead press[b]	1	8-12	2/4
7. Low back	1	8-12	2/4
8. Abdominal	1	8-12	2/4
9. 4-way neck[b]	1	8-12	2/4

[a]Up and down in seconds.

[b]New exercises this week.

Major muscle group	Machine
1. Quadriceps	Leg press
2. Hamstrings	Leg press
3. Hip adductors	Hip adductor
4. Hip abductors	Hip abductor
5. Pectoralis major	Vertical chest
6. Latissimus dorsi	Compound row
7. Deltoids	Overhead press
8. Biceps	Compound row
9. Triceps	Vertical chest Overhead press
10. Low back	Low back
11. Abdominals	Abdominal
12. Neck	4-way neck

Age group	Overhead press[a]	Neck flexion[a]	Neck extension[a]
20-29			
Males	50.0	45.0	50.0
Females	35.0	40.0	35.0
30-39			
Males	47.5	42.5	47.5
Females	32.5	27.5	32.5
40-49			
Males	45.0	40.0	45.0
Females	30.0	25.0	30.0
50-59			
Males	42.5	37.5	42.5
Females	27.5	22.5	27.5
60-69			
Males	40.0	35.0	40.0
Females	25.0	20.0	25.0
70-79			
Males	37.5	32.5	37.5
Females	20.0	20.0	22.5

[a]Weight load in pounds.

Exercise order	Training sets	Training repetitions	Training speed[a]
1. Leg press	1	8-12	2/4
2. Hip adductor	1	8-12	2/4
3. Hip abductor	1	8-12	2/4
4. Vertical chest	1	8-12	2/4
5. Compound row	1	8-12	2/4
6. Overhead press	1	8-12	2/4
7. Biceps curl[b]	1	8-12	2/4
8. Triceps extension[b]	1	8-12	2/4
9. Low back	1	8-12	2/4
10. Abdominal	1	8-12	2/4
11. 4-way neck	1	8-12	2/4

[a]Up and down in seconds.

[b]New exercises this week.

Major muscle group	Machine
1. Quadriceps	Leg press
2. Hamstrings	Leg press
3. Hip adductors	Hip adductor
4. Hip abductors	Hip abductor
5. Pectoralis major	Vertical chest
6. Latissimus dorsi	Compound row
7. Deltoids	Overhead press
8. Biceps	Compound row Biceps curl
9. Triceps	Vertical chest Overhead press Triceps extension
10. Low back	Low back
11. Abdominals	Abdominal
12. Neck	4-way neck

Age group	Biceps curl[a]	Triceps extension[a]
20-29		
Males	60.0	60.0
Females	32.5	32.5
30-39		
Males	55.0	55.0
Females	30.0	30.0
40-49		
Males	50.0	50.0
Females	27.5	27.5
50-59		
Males	45.0	45.0
Females	25.0	25.0
60-69		
Males	40.0	40.0
Females	22.5	22.5
70-79		
Males	35.0	35.0
Females	20.0	20.0

[a]Weight load in pounds.

Exercise order	Training sets	Training repetitions	Training speed[a]
1. Leg extension[b]	1	8-12	2/4
2. Seated leg curl[b]	1	8-12	2/4
3. Leg press	1	8-12	2/4
4. Hip adductor	1	8-12	2/4
5. Hip abductor	1	8-12	2/4
6. Vertical chest	1	8-12	2/4
7. Compound row	1	8-12	2/4
8. Overhead press	1	8-12	2/4
9. Biceps curl	1	8-12	2/4
10. Triceps extension	1	8-12	2/4
11. Low back	1	8-12	2/4
12. Abdominal	1	8-12	2/4
13. 4-way neck	1	8-12	2/4

[a]Up and down in seconds.

[b]New exercises this week.

Major muscle group	Machine
1. Quadriceps	Leg press Leg extension
2. Hamstrings	Leg press Seated leg curl
3. Hip adductors	Hip adductor
4. Hip abductors	Hip abductor
5. Pectoralis major	Vertical chest
6. Latissimus dorsi	Compound row
7. Deltoids	Overhead press
8. Biceps	Compound row Biceps curl
9. Triceps	Vertical chest Overhead press Triceps extension
10. Low back	Low back
11. Abdominals	Abdominal
12. Neck	4-way neck

Age group	Leg extension[a]	Seated leg curl[a]
20-29		
Males	70.0	70.0
Females	42.5	42.5
30-39		
Males	65.0	65.0
Females	40.0	40.0
40-49		
Males	60.0	60.0
Females	37.5	37.5
50-59		
Males	55.0	55.0
Females	35.0	35.0
60-69		
Males	50.0	50.0
Females	32.5	32.5
70-79		
Males	45.0	45.0
Females	30.0	30.0

[a]Weight load in pounds.

Exercise order	Training sets	Training repetitions	Training speed[a]
1. Leg extension	1	8-12	2/4
2. Seated leg curl	1	8-12	2/4
3. Leg press	1	8-12	2/4
4. Hip adductor	1	8-12	2/4
5. Hip abductor	1	8-12	2/4
6. Vertical chest	1	8-12	2/4
7. Compound row	1	8-12	2/4
8. Overhead press	1	8-12	2/4
9. Biceps curl	1	8-12	2/4
10. Triceps extension	1	8-12	2/4
11. Low back	1	8-12	2/4
12. Abdominal	1	8-12	2/4
13. 4-way neck	1	8-12	2/4
14. Chin/dip[b]	1	8-12	2/4

[a]Up and down in seconds. [b]New exercises this week.

Major muscle group	Machine
1. Quadriceps	Leg press Leg extension
2. Hamstrings	Leg press Seated leg curl
3. Hip adductors	Hip adductor
4. Hip abductors	Hip abductor
5. Pectoralis major	Vertical chest Weight-assisted chin/dip
6. Latissimus dorsi	Compound row Weight-assisted chin/dip
7. Deltoids	Overhead press
8. Biceps	Compound row Biceps curl Weight-assisted chin/dip
9. Triceps	Vertical chest Overhead press Triceps extension Weight-assisted chin/dip
10. Low back	Low back
11. Abdominals	Abdominal
12. Neck	4-way neck

Age group	Chin-up[a]	Bar dip[a]
20-29		
Males	40.0	40.0
Females	55.0	55.0
30-39		
Males	45.0	45.0
Females	60.0	60.0
40-49		
Males	50.0	50.0
Females	65.0	65.0
50-59		
Males	55.0	55.0
Females	70.0	70.0
60-69		
Males	60.0	60.0
Females	75.0	75.0
70-79		
Males	65.0	65.0
Females	80.0	80.0

[a]Weight load in pounds.

Exercise order	Training sets	Training repetitions	Training speed[a]
1. Leg extension	1	8-12	2/4
2. Seated leg curl	1	8-12	2/4
3. Leg press	1	8-12	2/4
4. Hip adductor	1	8-12	2/4
5. Hip abductor	1	8-12	2/4
6. Pec dec[b]	1	8-12	2/4
7. Super pullover[b]	1	8-12	2/4
8. Lateral raise[b]	1	8-12	2/4
9. Biceps curl	1	8-12	2/4
10. Triceps extension	1	8-12	2/4
11. Low back	1	8-12	2/4
12. Abdominal	1	8-12	2/4
13. 4-way neck	1	8-12	2/4
14. Chin/dip	1	8-12	2/4

[a]Up and down in seconds. [b]New exercises this week.

Major muscle group	Machine
1. Quadriceps	Leg press / Leg extension
2. Hamstrings	Leg press / Seated leg curl
3. Hip adductors	Hip adductor
4. Hip abductors	Hip abductor
5. Pectoralis major	Pec dec / Weight-assisted chin/dip
6. Latissimus dorsi	Super pullover / Weight-assisted chin/dip
7. Deltoids	Lateral raise
8. Biceps	Biceps curl / Weight-assisted chin/dip
9. Triceps	Triceps extension / Weight-assisted chin/dip
10. Low back	Low back
11. Abdominals	Abdominal
12. Neck	4-way neck

Age group	Pec dec[a]	Super pullover[a]	Lateral raise[a]
20-29			
Males	60.0	65.0	55.0
Females	37.5	40.0	35.0
30-39			
Males	57.5	62.5	52.5
Females	35.0	37.5	32.5
40-49			
Males	55.0	60.0	50.0
Females	32.5	35.0	30.0
50-59			
Males	52.5	57.5	47.5
Females	30.0	32.5	27.5
60-69			
Males	50.0	55.0	45.0
Females	27.5	30.0	25.0
70-79			
Males	47.5	52.5	42.5
Females	25.0	27.5	22.5

[a]Weight load in pounds.

Conclusion of Two-Month Training Program

After completing eight weeks of progressive strength and endurance workouts with a variety of resistance exercises, you should have a reasonably high level of confidence and competence in your training ability. You have succeeded in the most challenging phase of your muscle conditioning program.

At this point, you may continue your present strength training protocol or you may periodically change the exercises for enhanced effectiveness and motivational purposes. You may also choose to perform fewer exercises or more exercises depending on your training objectives and time availability. Just remember to address the major muscle groups and to work opposing muscles for comprehensive conditioning and muscle balance. Also, be sure to increase the exercise resistance whenever you complete 12 good repetitions, as this is the key to training intensity and continued progress.

You may also continue to alternate endurance exercises or you may select the ones that you find most satisfying. Just remember to apply the basic training principles to all of your aerobic workouts.

Free Weight Training

The table on page 192 presents the recommended free weight exercises for an initial two-month training period. Like the machine progression, you begin with three basic exercises and systematically add and substitute new exercises each week of training. Use an exercise resistance that permits 8 to 12 properly performed repetitions. When 12 repetitions can be completed, increase the weight load by approximately 5 percent.

Summary

After two months of sensible and progressive strength and endurance exercise, you should notice major improvements in your muscular and cardiovascular fitness as well as in your body composition and physical appearance. You may continue with these programs indefinitely, or you may change exercise protocols periodically as you continue training. The following chapter provides sample strength and endurance exercise programs for an additional four months of training.

Free Weight Regimen
Recommended program of free weight training for first two months

Week	Exercises	
1	Barbell squat[a]	
	Barbell bench press[a]	
	Dumbbell bent row[a]	
2	Barbell squat	Trunk extension[a]
	Barbell bench press	Trunk curl[a]
	Dumbbell bent row	
3	Barbell squat	Dumbbell press[a]
	Barbell bench press	Trunk extension
	Dumbbell bent row	Trunk curl
4	Barbell squat	Barbell curl[a]
	Barbell bench press	Triceps pressdown[a]
	Dumbbell bent row	Trunk extension
	Dumbbell press	Trunk curl
5	Barbell squat	Barbell curl
	Dumbbell lunge[a]	Triceps pressdown
	Barbell bench press	Barbell shoulder shrug[a]
	Pullover[a]	Trunk extension
	Dumbbell press	Trunk curl
6	Barbell squat	Dumbbell overhead triceps extension[a]
	Dumbbell lunge	Barbell shoulder shrug
	Barbell incline press[a]	Trunk extension
	Pulldown[a]	Trunk curl
	Dumbbell lateral raise[a]	Chin-up[a]
	Dumbbell preacher curl[a]	Bar dip[a]
7	Barbell squat	Dumbbell preacher curl
	Dumbbell lunge	Dumbbell overhead triceps extension
	Dumbbell bench fly[a]	Dumbbell shoulder shrug
	Barbell incline press	Trunk extension
	Dumbbell pullover[a]	Twisting knee-lift trunk curl[a]
	Pulldown	Chin-up
	Dumbbell lateral raise	Bar dip
8	Barbell squat	Dumbbell preacher curl
	Dumbbell lunge	Dumbbell triceps kickback[a]
	Dumbbell step-up[a]	Dumbbell shoulder shrug
	Dumbbell bench fly	Trunk extension
	Dumbbell incline press	Twisting knee-lift trunk curl
	Dumbbell pullover	Chin-up
	Pulldown	Bar dip
	Dumbbell lateral raise	

[a]New exercises this week.

Six-Month Training Programs

Now that you have experienced two months of strength and endurance exercise, you have a pretty good idea of how to integrate exercises to progress in a systematic manner. However, in case you desire further direction for attaining higher levels of muscular and cardiovascular fitness, you may incorporate the following suggested programs for the next four months. After you finish these routines, you will have completed six months of purposeful exercise, and you should be well on your way to a lifetime of fitness.

This chapter presents four more months of combined strength and endurance exercise programs with a different emphasis each month to maximize physical and mental responsiveness to the training protocols. These programs are sound, safe, and sensible, but you may choose to alter them according to your personal abilities and objectives.

Month Three

The emphasis in the third month will be on substituting different exercises for both your strength and endurance training programs. Your strength training guidelines remain the same: one set of 8 to 12 repetitions performed at a slow movement speed through a full movement range, exhaling during each lifting action and inhaling during each lowering action. Whenever you complete 12 good repetitions, increase the exercise resistance by at least 5 percent.

Program 10.1 presents the strength exercise changes as you enter your third month of training. You will note a pre-exhaustion approach to your upper body muscles, whereby a rotary exercise is followed by a linear exercise to enhance the training effect on each target muscle group.

Program 10.2 presents the endurance changes as you enter your third month of training. You will perform about 30 minutes of aerobic activity, three days a week, at an effort level that raises your heart rate to about 75 percent of maximum.

Present exercise order	New exercise order	Major muscle groups
1. Leg extension	1. Leg extension	Quadriceps
2. Seated leg curl	2. Prone leg curl[a]	Hamstrings
3. Leg press	3. Leg press	Quadriceps, hamstrings
4. Hip adductor	4. Pec dec	Pectoralis major
5. Hip abductor	5. Vertical chest[a]	Pectoralis major, triceps
6. Pec dec	6. Super pullover	Latissimus dorsi
7. Super pullover	7. Lat pulldown[a]	Latissimus dorsi, biceps
8. Lateral raise	8. Lateral raise	Deltoids
9. Biceps curl	9. Overhead press[a]	Deltoids, triceps
10. Triceps extension	10. Biceps curl	Biceps
11. Low back	11. Assisted chin-up	Biceps, latissimus dorsi
12. Abdominal curl	12. Triceps extension	Triceps
13. 4-way neck	13. Assisted bar dip	Triceps, pectoralis major
14. Assisted chin-up	14. Rotary torso[a]	Obliques, rectus abdominis
15. Assisted bar dip	15. 4-way neck	Neck extensors, neck flexors

[a]New exercises this month.

Week	Day	Exercise	Time	Effort level
1	Monday	Cycling	30 min.	75% max. heart rate
	Wednesday	Walking	30 min.	75% max. heart rate
	Friday	Stepping	30 min.	75% max. heart rate
2	Monday	Rowing	30 min.	75% max. heart rate
	Wednesday	Cycling	30 min.	75% max. heart rate
	Friday	Walking	30 min.	75% max. heart rate
3	Monday	Stepping	30 min.	75% max. heart rate
	Wednesday	Rowing	30 min.	75% max. heart rate
	Friday	Cycling	30 min.	75% max. heart rate
4	Monday	Walking	30 min.	75% max. heart rate
	Wednesday	Stepping	30 min.	75% max. heart rate
	Friday	Rowing	30 min.	75% max. heart rate

Month Four

After three months of regular and progressive strength and endurance exercise, you should be able to perform more challenging training protocols that further increase your muscular and cardiovascular fitness. Your approach this month is higher-intensity training in which you work harder for fewer repetitions (strength exercise) and shorter durations (endurance exercise).

Program 10.3 indicates the recommended changes in your strength workouts. You will perform the same exercises but with more resistance and fewer repetitions. Continue to do one set of each exercise at a slow movement speed and through a full movement range.

Program 10.4 shows the suggested modifications to your endurance workouts. Although you will perform the same basic aerobic activities, you will work at a higher effort level (approximately 80 percent of your maximum heart rate) for less time (about 20 minutes) each exercise session (which may necessitate replacing treadmill walking with jogging). Continue to train three days a week, which should allow you to recover completely between successive workouts.

PROGRAM 10.3	MONTH 4	
Exercise order	**Exercise resistance**[a]	**Exercise repetitions**
1. Leg extension	Increase 5-15 lb.	6-10
2. Prone leg curl	Increase 5-15 lb.	6-10
3. Leg press	Increase 10-30 lb.	6-10
4. Pec dec	Increase 5-10 lb.	6-10
5. Vertical chest	Increase 5-15 lb.	6-10
6. Super pullover	Increase 5-10 lb.	6-10
7. Lat pulldown	Increase 5-15 lb.	6-10
8. Lateral raise	Increase 5-10 lb.	6-10
9. Overhead press	Increase 5-15 lb.	6-10
10. Biceps curl	Increase 5-10 lb.	6-10
11. Assisted chin-up	Increase 5-10 lb.	6-10
12. Triceps extension	Increase 5-10 lb.	6-10
13. Assisted bar dip	Increase 5-10 lb.	6-10
14. Rotary torso	Increase 5-10 lb.	6-10
15. 4-way neck	Increase 5-10 lb.	6-10

[a]Increase over last month's training weight loads.

PROGRAM 10.4		MONTH 4		
Week	**Day**	**Exercise**	**Time**	**Effort level**
1	Monday	Cycling	20 min.	80% max. heart rate
	Wednesday	Jogging	20 min.	80% max. heart rate
	Friday	Stepping	20 min.	80% max. heart rate
2	Monday	Rowing	20 min.	80% max. heart rate
	Wednesday	Cycling	20 min.	80% max. heart rate
	Friday	Jogging	20 min.	80% max. heart rate
3	Monday	Stepping	20 min.	80% max. heart rate
	Wednesday	Rowing	20 min.	80% max. heart rate
	Friday	Cycling	20 min.	80% max. heart rate
4	Monday	Jogging	20 min.	80% max. heart rate
	Wednesday	Stepping	20 min.	80% max. heart rate
	Friday	Rowing	20 min.	80% max. heart rate

Month Five

Last month provided a higher-intensity approach to muscular and cardiovascular training, which should have produced higher levels of overall physical fitness. However, you should vary your exercise protocol periodically to prevent both overtraining and burnout. This month you will swing the pendulum in the other direction to provide a different training stimulus and foster continued fitness improvement. Your strength training program features more repetitions with less resistance, and your endurance training program requires longer periods of lower-intensity aerobic activity.

Program 10.5 presents the new strength training recommendations, using the same exercises as last month. You will continue to perform one set of each exercise with controlled movement speed and full movement range, exhaling during each lifting action and inhaling during each lowering action.

Program 10.6 provides you with a similar program of endurance workouts but with longer training durations. To permit completion of the extended exercise sessions without discomfort or discouragement, the training intensity has been reduced accordingly. You should be able to complete 40-minute training sessions at the lower work levels (approximately 70 percent of maximum heart rate), but you may need to substitute treadmill walking for jogging.

PROGRAM 10.5	MONTH 5	

Exercise order	Exercise resistance[a]	Exercise repetitions
1. Leg extension	Decrease 10-25 lb.	10-14
2. Prone leg curl	Decrease 10-25 lb.	10-14
3. Leg press	Decrease 15-35 lb.	10-14
4. Pec dec	Decrease 10-15 lb.	10-14
5. Vertical chest	Decrease 10-20 lb.	10-14
6. Super pullover	Decrease 10-15 lb.	10-14
7. Lat pulldown	Decrease 10-20 lb.	10-14
8. Lateral raise	Decrease 10-15 lb.	10-14
9. Overhead press	Decrease 10-20 lb.	10-14
10. Biceps curl	Decrease 10-15 lb.	10-14
11. Assisted chin-up	Decrease 10-15 lb.	10-14
12. Triceps extension	Decrease 10-15 lb.	10-14
13. Assisted bar dip	Decrease 10-15 lb.	10-14
14. Rotary torso	Decrease 10-15 lb.	10-14
15. 4-way neck	Decrease 10-15 lb.	10-14

[a]Decrease from last month's training weight loads.

PROGRAM 10.6	MONTH 5			

Week	Day	Exercise	Time	Effort level
1	Monday	Cycling	40 min.	70% max. heart rate
	Wednesday	Walking	40 min.	70% max. heart rate
	Friday	Stepping	40 min.	70% max. heart rate
2	Monday	Rowing	40 min.	70% max. heart rate
	Wednesday	Cycling	40 min.	70% max. heart rate
	Friday	Walking	40 min.	70% max. heart rate
3	Monday	Stepping	40 min.	70% max. heart rate
	Wednesday	Rowing	40 min.	70% max. heart rate
	Friday	Cycling	40 min.	70% max. heart rate
4	Monday	Walking	40 min.	70% max. heart rate
	Wednesday	Stepping	40 min.	70% max. heart rate
	Friday	Rowing	40 min.	70% max. heart rate

Month Six

You are ready to begin your sixth month of strength and endurance exercise, and you will soon complete a half-year of physical conditioning. You should have attained relatively high levels of muscular and cardiovascular fitness, and a change in training protocols is in order. This month you will initiate some more advanced workouts, adding breakdown repetitions to some of the strength exercises and performing interval training in the endurance sessions. Program 10.7 provides a somewhat different battery of strength exercises as well as recommendations for extended set training using three post-fatigue breakdown repetitions. You will perform one set of each exercise with a resistance that fatigues the target muscle group in 8 to 12 controlled repetitions (slow movement speed and full movement range). Immediately after reaching muscle fatigue with your initial weight load, breakdown repetitions should be completed as indicated with a reduced resistance.

Program 10.8 presents an interval training approach to your aerobic workouts. Alternating higher-effort and lower-effort exercise segments represents a more challenging training session and results in greater cardiovascular benefits. You will progress from shorter to longer intervals as well as to reduced recovery intervals as you become better conditioned. Be sure to spend the recommended amount of time warming up and cooling down when doing interval training workouts. You may use any of the aerobic activities you choose for interval training sessions.

PROGRAM 10.7	MONTH 6	
Exercise order	**Pre-fatigue training protocol**	**Post-fatigue training protocol**[a]
1. Hip adduction	1 set × 8-12 reps	3 reps with 15-25 lb. less wt.
2. Hip abduction	1 set × 8-12 reps	3 reps with 15-25 lb. less wt.
3. Leg press	1 set × 8-12 reps	3 reps with 30-50 lb. less wt.
4. Chest press	1 set × 8-12 reps	3 reps with 10-20 lb. less wt.
5. Compound row	1 set × 8-12 reps	3 reps with 10-20 lb. less wt.
6. Incline press	1 set × 8-12 reps	3 reps with 10-20 lb. less wt.
7. Biceps curl	1 set × 8-12 reps	3 reps with 10-15 lb. less wt.
8. Triceps extension	1 set × 8-12 reps	3 reps with 10-15 lb. less wt.
9. Low back	1 set × 8-12 reps	no post-fatigue reps
10. Abdominal	1 set × 8-12 reps	3 reps with 10-20 lb. less wt.
11. 4-way neck	1 set × 8-12 reps	no post-fatigue reps
12. Assisted chin-up	1 set × 8-12 reps	no post-fatigue reps
13. Assisted bar dip	1 set × 8-12 reps	no post-fatigue reps

[a]Take as little time as possible between your initial training set and your post-fatigue repetitions with the reduced weight load.

PROGRAM 10.8			MONTH 6
Week	**Warm-up**	**Cool-down**	**Interval training protocol[a]**
1	4 min.	4 min.	2 min. at 70% max. heart rate
			2 min. at 80% max. heart rate
			2 min. at 70% max. heart rate
			2 min. at 80% max. heart rate
			2 min. at 70% max. heart rate
			2 min. at 80% max. heart rate
			2 min. at 70% max. heart rate
			2 min. at 80% max. heart rate
2	4 min.	4 min.	3 min. at 70% max. heart rate
			3 min. at 80% max. heart rate
			3 min. at 70% max. heart rate
			3 min. at 80% max. heart rate
			3 min. at 70% max. heart rate
			3 min. at 80% max. heart rate
3	4 min.	4 min.	3 min. at 70% max. heart rate
			4 min. at 80% max. heart rate
			3 min. at 70% max. heart rate
			4 min. at 80% max. heart rate
			3 min. at 70% max. heart rate
			4 min. at 80% max. heart rate
4	4 min.	4 min.	2 min. at 70% max. heart rate
			4 min. at 80% max. heart rate
			2 min. at 70% max. heart rate
			4 min. at 80% max. heart rate
			2 min. at 70% max. heart rate
			4 min. at 80% max. heart rate

[a]Use any endurance activity you choose for your interval training workouts.

Summary

The sample six-month training programs provide models for gradually increasing muscular and cardiovascular fitness by performing progressively more challenging strength and endurance workouts. Throughout these months of more advanced exercise, the basic training principles remain the same. All of the strength exercises should be executed in proper form with emphasis on controlled movement speed and full movement range. Likewise, all of the aerobic activities should be performed with correct technique and at the appropriate effort level.

Recommendations for Best Results

Although you may substitute exercises and personalize the training procedures over the six-month conditioning period, be sure to use the following guidelines to maximize fitness development and to minimize injury risk:

- Warm up before and cool down after each workout.
- Progress in a gradual and systematic manner from one training session to the next.
- Train within your physical abilities, and avoid the temptation to do too much too soon.
- Maintain a regular exercise schedule because training consistency is the key to fitness improvement.
- Keep careful records of each training session for purposes of appropriate progression and personal motivation.

Fitness Program Design and Evaluation

Okay, you understand the training principles and procedures for developing muscular strength and cardiovascular endurance. But how do you put everything together into an integrated program of strength and endurance exercise?

Arrangement of Activities

Does it matter which activity you do first? The answer is a solid no. Depending on your personal fitness goals, the order of the activities has little effect on the training results as long as you follow the recommended exercise guidelines.[1,2,3] Generally, endurance athletes should perform endurance exercise first and strength athletes should do strength exercise first. But if your objective is overall physical fitness, the following basic exercise procedure is recommended: Begin with a progressive warm-up for a smooth transition from rest to vigorous activity. Next, do your endurance exercise, followed by your strength exercise. Finally, gradually cool down to restore normal blood circulation and resting metabolism. This is also a good time for a few stretches to finish your training session feeling loose and relaxed.

How do you know how many workouts to do each week? It's easy! To avoid overtraining when combining strength and endurance exercise, stick to a schedule of three days per week. For example, you could train on Mondays, Wednesdays, and Fridays and rest the remainder of the week. If your emphasis is on cardiovascular conditioning, you may increase the number of aerobic workouts, but the extra training could limit your strength development. If your emphasis is on muscular conditioning, you may work harder but not more frequently because your muscles require about two days for strength-building processes to be completed. If your goal is an injury-free exercise program that produces a high level of physical fitness, it's hard to beat a three-day-a-week combined strength and endurance program.

A combined program does not have to take an unreasonable amount of time. Both the sample strength training sessions and the sample endurance training sessions given in chapter 9 take about 25 to 30 minutes each. A 10-week study comparing three training groups demonstrated excellent results from a three-day-a-week combination program.[4] The combined strength and endurance group developed as much strength as the strength-only group (see figure 11.1) and almost as much endurance as the endurance-only group (see figure 11.2). The three-day-a-week program of combined strength and endurance exercise effectively and efficiently achieved maximum gains in muscular strength and near-maximum gains in cardiovascular endurance.

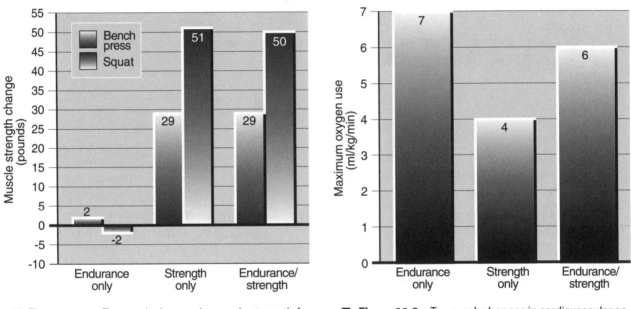

■ **Figure 11.1** Ten-week changes in muscle strength for three training groups.

■ **Figure 11.2** Ten-week changes in cardiovascular endurance for three training groups.

Based on the programs described in chapter 9, program 11.1 shows a sample combination training program with approximate time segments for all of the exercise components. Although you may make periodic changes in your exercise program, the one-hour combined activity format is an effective and efficient approach for reaching high levels of muscular and cardiovascular fitness.

Stretching

Most of us agree that stretching exercises are useful for enhancing joint flexibility and overall physical fitness, but we do not always find time for this part of our exercise program. If you try to do about 30 minutes of strength exercise and 30 minutes of endurance exercise each session, there is little room in a one-hour workout for stretching.

PROGRAM 11.1   Sample Protocol for General Exercise Session

Time frame	General activity	Specific exercises
0-5 min.	Warm-up	Easy cycling at 60% max. heart rate
5-20 min.	Endurance exercise	Interval cycling alternating 3 min. at 70% max. heart rate and 3 min. at 80% max. heart rate
20-25 min.	Cool-down	Easy cycling at 60% max. heart rate
25-55 min.	Strength exercise	One set each of leg extensions, seated leg curls, hip adduction, hip abduction, chest presses, lat pulldowns, overhead presses, biceps curls, triceps extensions, low back extensions, abdominal curls, and 4-way neck exercises
55-60 min.	Cool-down and stretching	Hamstring stretch, low back stretch, shoulder stretch, and calf stretch

Although properly performed strength training alone improves joint flexibility, you still should do stretching exercises. The key muscle–joint structures that should be addressed in a stretching program include the following:

- Calf muscles, which cross the ankle and knee joints
- Hamstring muscles, which cross the knee and hip joints
- Low back muscles, which lie on both sides of the vertebral column
- Rotator cuff muscles, which surround the shoulder joints

Although some of these muscles are large and others are small, the basic stretching procedure is about the same. Gradually stretch the target muscle until it is comfortably lengthened, then hold that position for at least 20 seconds. This gentle approach reduces the risk of overstretching and maintains the stretched position long enough to produce positive muscle adaptations. If you have time, it may help to perform each stretch twice.

You may do stretching exercises while warming up or cooling down, or both. The cool-down is preferred for two reasons. First, your muscles are warmer and more stretchable after your workout. Second, stretching exercises serve as an excellent transition from activity to rest, helping you leave your training session feeling relaxed rather than tight.

Another time-saving alternative is to stretch the muscles just worked immediately after each strength exercise. Research has shown almost 20 percent greater strength gains when you combine your strength exercises and stretching.[5] For example, the leg extension exercise may be followed by a 20-second stretch for the quadriceps muscles, the seated leg curl exercise may be followed by a 20-second stretch for the hamstring muscles, and so on.

"Big Four" Stretches

Although you may include additional exercises if you like, the following "big four" recommended stretches are ideal for developing flexibility: the step stretch, the figure 4 stretch, the letter T stretch, and the doorway stretch. When performed properly, these stretches should enhance flexibility in your key muscle–joint structures.

Step Stretch

The step stretch targets the calf muscles in the lower leg. Because these muscles cross both the knee and ankle joints, keep your knee straight as you perform this exercise. Stand with your right foot fully on the step and your left foot half on and half off the step. Place one hand on the handrail or wall for balance. Gently shift your weight to your left foot and allow your left heel to slowly drop downward. As soon as your left calf muscles feel comfortably stretched, hold the position for at least 20 seconds. Change foot positions and repeat the same procedure for your right calf muscles (see figure 11.3).

Figure 4 Stretch

The figure 4 stretch resembles the number it is named after. Although it actually addresses several muscles, you should feel the greatest stretch in the hamstrings at the back of the thighs (see figure 11.4). Begin by sitting on the floor with your left leg straight and your right leg bent at the knee so that your right foot touches your left thigh. Slowly reach your left hand toward your left foot until your hamstrings feel comfortably stretched. At this point, grasp your foot, ankle, or lower leg and hold the stretched position for at least 20 seconds. Change leg positions and repeat the same procedure for your right hamstrings. You should also feel some stretching effects in your calf, hip, lower back, and shoulder muscles as you do the figure 4 stretch.

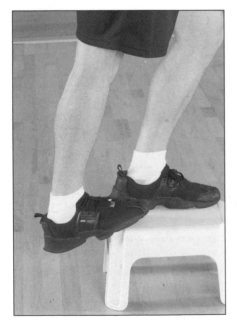

■ **Figure 11.3** Step stretch.

■ **Figure 11.4** Figure 4 stretch.

Letter T Stretch

As you may imagine, this stretch resembles the letter *T*. It is designed to stretch the lower back and hip muscles from a fully supported position (see figure 11.5). Start by lying face-up on the floor with your arms straight out to the sides in a T position. Slowly lift your left leg upward, then cross it over so that your left foot is near your right hand. Hold this comfortably stretched position for at least 20 seconds. Return to the starting position and repeat the same procedure with your right leg. As you carefully cross your leg over your body, do your best to keep the other leg straight.

■ **Figure 11.5** Letter T stretch.

Doorway Stretch

This two-part stretching exercise targets some of the rotator cuff muscles in the shoulder. Before beginning the doorway stretch, you may want to do some very slow arm circles to loosen up your shoulder joints. Part one of the doorway stretch begins by standing in a doorway with your right arm across your body and grasping the left doorframe at about shoulder level (see figure 11.6). Gently turn your body to the right until your rear shoulder muscles feel comfortably stretched. Hold this position for at least 20 seconds. Part two begins by grasping the right doorframe with your right arm at about shoulder level. Gently turn your body to the left until your front shoulder muscles feel comfortably stretched. Hold this position for a minimum of 20 seconds. Repeat these two stretches with your left arm.

Keep in mind that slow and controlled stretching is critical for safety and success. A lack of muscle tension and a relaxed sensation should characterize the stretching process. Always avoid trying too hard and

■ **Figure 11.6** Doorway stretch.

stretching into the discomfort zone. The "big four" stretching sequence is an ideal way to conclude your exercise sessions, leaving you feeling invigorated rather than exhausted.

Evaluating Your Progress

Your physical fitness program should be pleasant, satisfying, and rewarding. As a result of your exercise efforts, you should feel, function, and look better. Still, many of us appreciate objective assessments of our progress as well as norms by which we can evaluate our personal fitness. As explained earlier in the book, four specific components related to overall physical fitness are body composition, muscular strength, joint flexibility, and cardiovascular endurance. These are key areas to examine when judging your overall progress.

Body Composition

Body composition refers to your ratio of fat weight to lean weight and is usually reported as percent body fat. Men should be less than 15 percent fat weight and more than 85 percent lean weight, while women should be less than 25 percent fat weight and more than 75 percent lean weight. Your body composition can be assessed very accurately at most fitness centers by means of skinfold calipers or bioelectrical impedance technology.

What if you are overweight but don't have access to body composition assessment equipment? You can still evaluate personal improvements in this area by taking periodic waist measurements. If you are male, stand "tall" and place a measuring tape around your waist just above your belt. At a normal rate of body composition improvement, you should see about a one-half-inch reduction in your waist measurement each month of training. If you are female, stand "tall" and place a measuring tape around the largest circumference of your hips. At a normal rate of body composition improvement, you should note about a one-half-inch reduction in your hip measurement each month of training.

Muscular Strength

Muscular strength is related to body weight and exercise program. That is, larger individuals are typically stronger than smaller individuals, and trained muscles are usually stronger than untrained muscles. For this reason, be sure to use strength assessments that adjust for body weight and address major muscle groups such as the quadriceps.

Perhaps the best muscular strength assessment is the YMCA Leg Extension Test, which is based on data from over 900 men and women.[6] The YMCA Leg Extension Test uses your 10-repetition maximum weight load, so it is a safe strength assessment with a low risk of injury. And because it addresses the large and regularly used quadriceps, it is a practical test of muscular strength. The YMCA test also provides fair strength comparisons for men and women of various sizes because it evaluates strength relative to body weight.

If appropriate testing equipment is not available, you can evaluate your strength improvement by periodically comparing your exercise weight loads. Generally speaking, your exercise resistance should increase about 45 percent during the first two months of training and about 15 percent during the next two months of training. After that, a 5 percent strength improvement every two months is excellent. For

YMCA Leg Extension Test

■ Select a weight load on the Nautilus leg extension machine that is about 30 to 40 percent of your body weight.

■ Perform 10 repetitions in the following manner:

　1. Lift the roller pad in two seconds to full knee extension.

　2. Hold the fully contracted position for one second.

　3. Lower the roller pad in four seconds until the weight stack lightly touches.

■ If you complete 10 repetitions, rest 2 minutes, select a weight load that is about 50 percent of your body weight, and perform 10 repetitions.

■ Continue testing this way until you find the heaviest weight load that you can do for 10 repetitions.

■ Divide this weight load by your body weight to determine your strength quotient.

■ Locate your strength quotient in the appropriate strength and fitness classification.

Strength quotient classifications		
Muscle strength	Men	Women
Low	49% body weight or below	39% body weight or below
Below average	50-59% body weight	40-49% body weight
Average	60-69% body weight	50-59% body weight
Above average	70-79% body weight	60-69% body weight
High	80% body weight or above	70% body weight or above

According to this assessment technique, a 120-pound woman who performs 10 leg extensions with 60 pounds has a strength quotient of 50 percent—average strength in her quadriceps.

example, if you begin with a leg press of 100 pounds, you should be able to leg press about 145 pounds after two months of training, approximately 165 pounds after four months of training, and almost 175 pounds after six months of training.

Joint Flexibility

Joint flexibility refers to the movement range of a given joint structure. It is highly specific and may vary considerably from joint to joint. Because poor hip and trunk flexibility may be related to low back problems, this is the area most frequently evaluated in flexibility tests. If you have good hip and trunk flexibility, you should be able to touch your toes without bending your knees. To avoid back strain, perform this assessment in a sitting—rather than a standing—position.

To evaluate your hip and trunk flexibility, sit on the floor with a yardstick between your legs, lining up the 15-inch mark with your heels (see figure 11.7). With your knees straight, reach forward as far as possible without straining. If you can touch the 15-inch mark, you are reasonably flexible in the hip and trunk area. If you cannot stretch this far, an inch a month increase is an excellent rate of improvement. Although you may be able to reach beyond your toes, don't try to develop extreme flexibility, as excessive joint mobility may raise your risk of injury.

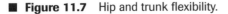

■ **Figure 11.7**   Hip and trunk flexibility.

Cardiovascular Endurance

Cardiovascular endurance is primarily a measure of your ability to perform aerobic activity. Most fitness centers offer cardiovascular endurance assessments using cycle, treadmill, or step tests.

If you do not have access to supervised evaluation techniques, you may measure your cardiovascular progress in less formal ways. For a general assessment, periodically monitor your resting heart rate. Your resting heart rate typically slows down as your cardiovascular condition improves, so a progressive reduction in your resting heart rate indicates an effective endurance training program.

Another assessment procedure is to periodically compare your training heart rate at a given exercise level. As your cardiovascular fitness increases, your training heart rate at the same work level should decrease. For example, during the first month of training, recumbent cycling at level 3 may raise your heart rate to 140 beats a minute. During the second month of training, this same workout may elevate your heart rate to only 132 beats a minute, and during the third month, to only 124 beats a minute.

These assessment techniques may provide more objective information about your fitness development. The most revealing feature of a successful exercise program, however, is your training regularity. Without question, the critical factor in reaching and maintaining a high level of physical fitness is your training consistency. Regular training sessions with gradual improvements give more overall benefits than an occasional outstanding workout.

Summary

A combination strength and endurance training program effectively improves both muscular and cardiovascular fitness. For best overall results, you should train three days a week and rest between exercise sessions. This encourages fitness development, giving the body time to adapt to physical changes between workouts and reducing your risk of injury. Although the activity order is a matter of personal preference, be sure to warm up before and cool down after each training session.

Periodically check your fitness progress with formal or informal assessment techniques. A well-designed exercise program should produce consistent improvements in your body composition, muscular strength, joint flexibility, and cardiovascular endurance. But the most important indicator of a physically productive and personally satisfying exercise program is your training regularity. You should look forward to each workout as a challenging and rewarding experience that is an essential part of your normal lifestyle.

Advanced Training Programs

Congratulations! You are now ready for more advanced training. At this point, you may be working hard but making few fitness gains. As you achieve higher levels of fitness, your rate of improvement gradually slows down, and you eventually reach a training plateau. Although lack of progress may be discouraging, it is simply a sign that you should change your exercise program. Of course, everyone has different genetic potential for physical development, so you should approach advanced training in a sensible manner.

Should you do more work to further increase your muscular strength and cardiovascular endurance? Not necessarily. Although more sets of strength exercise and longer periods of endurance exercise may be effective, this training approach poses two problems for most people.

First, more exercise sets and longer endurance sessions increase the training time, which is typically a limiting factor. Second, increasing the amount of exercise may lead to overtraining, fatigue, and injury—all of which are undesirable. A more practical approach to overcoming fitness plateaus is to increase the exercise intensity without significantly increasing the exercise duration. There are several effective and efficient methods for moving into an advanced strength training program.

Advanced Strength Training

After a certain period of training, muscles become less responsive to the regular workout routine, and a new exercise program is in order. As presented in chapter 5, the three best procedures for overcoming strength plateaus are the following:

1. Choose different exercises to address the same muscle groups. For example, replace the compound row exercise with the lat pulldown exercise for a different training stimulus to the latissimus dorsi and biceps muscles.

2. Change the training protocol by using different resistance–repetitions relationships. For example, perform 6 to 8 overhead presses with a heavier weight load instead of completing 10 to 12 overhead presses with a lighter weight load for a different training stimulus to the deltoid and triceps muscles.

3. Increase the exercise effort by using one or more of the high-intensity strength techniques. For example, extend each exercise set with breakdown, assisted, or pre-exhaustion training to increase muscle activation or extend each exercise repetition with slow-positive or slow-negative training to increase muscle activation.

This chapter provides sample high-intensity strength training programs based on the information discussed in chapter 5. A brief review of the high-intensity strength training protocols is presented in table 12.1.

When using high-intensity training techniques, be sure to leave sufficient recovery and building time between successive exercise sessions. The higher-effort workouts produce greater muscle stress and more tissue microtrauma, necessitating less frequent training sessions. Generally speaking, two high-intensity workouts per week are recommended to maximize strength development and minimize injury risk.

Table 12.1 Brief Descriptions of Basic High-Intensity Strength Training Protocols

Training procedure	Exercise example
Breakdown training	
At completion of the exercise set, reduce your resistance about 10 to 20% and perform a few post-fatigue repetitions.	Complete 10 to 12 leg extensions to fatigue with 100 lb. Immediately drop the weight load to 85 lb. and perform 2 to 4 additional repetitions to push the quadriceps muscles to a deeper level of fatigue.
Assisted training	
At completion of the exercise set, have your helper provide manual assistance on the lifting phase of a few post-fatigue repetitions.	Complete 10 to 12 leg curls to fatigue with 80 lb. Immediately perform 2 to 4 additional repetitions with manual assistance on the lifting phase to push the hamstring muscles to a deeper level of fatigue.
Pre-exhaustion training	
At completion of the first (rotary movement) exercise set, perform a second (linear movement) exercise set for the same target muscle group without resting between the successive exercises.	Complete 8 to 10 lateral raises to fatigue with 60 lb. Immediately perform 4 to 6 overhead presses to push the deltoid muscles to a deeper level of fatigue.
Slow positive-emphasis training	
Perform fewer repetitions at a slower speed, taking 10 sec. for each concentric muscle action and 4 sec. for each eccentric muscle action.	Complete 4 to 6 biceps curls, taking 10 sec. for each lifting movement and 4 sec. for each lowering movement.
Slow negative-emphasis training	
Perform fewer repetitions at a slower speed, taking 4 sec. for each concentric muscle action and 10 sec. for each eccentric muscle action.	Complete 4 to 6 triceps extensions, taking 4 sec. for each lifting movement and 10 sec. for each lowering movement.

You must also pay more attention to daily nutrition and nightly sleep when performing advanced strength training programs. Water and other healthy fluids (e.g., fruit juices, low-fat milk) are critically important because muscles are about 75 percent water. The other 25 percent of muscle tissue is protein, which may necessitate somewhat larger portions of protein-rich foods (e.g., chicken, fish, low-fat yogurt). Because the energy for high-intensity strength training comes primarily from carbohydrate sources, you may also need more grains, cereals, fruits, and vegetables (e.g., bagels, bananas, raisins).

Sleep experts tell us that the average adult needs approximately eight hours of sleep to function optimally in both physical and mental activities. Although it may not always be practical, high-intensity strength exercisers should attain at least this much sleep, and more if possible, on a nightly basis.

High-Intensity Strength Training Programs

You can design an almost unlimited number of high-intensity strength training programs by manipulating the numerous exercise variables. For three examples of basic high-intensity strength training protocols, please refer to tables 12.2, 12.3, and 12.4.

Keep in mind that advanced strength training requires a good balance between exercise effort and recovery period. Too little stimulus or too much rest may result in underachievement, whereas too much stimulus or too little rest may lead to overtraining. To maximize exercise benefits and minimize training risks, try to keep your work effort and recovery period in the shaded area shown in figure 12.1.

Table 12.2 Sample High-Intensity Strength Training Protocol Using Breakdown Training for Lower Body Exercises and Assisted Training for Upper Body Exercises

Exercise	Pre-fatigue resistance and repetitions	Post-fatigue resistance and repetitions
Leg extension	100 lb. × 10-12 reps	85 lb. × 2-4 reps
Leg curl	80 lb. × 10-12 reps	70 lb. × 2-4 reps
Hip adduction	120 lb. × 10-12 reps	100 lb. × 2-4 reps
Hip abduction	100 lb. × 10-12 reps	85 lb. × 2-4 reps
Leg press	200 lb. × 10-12 reps	170 lb. × 2-4 reps
Chest cross	90 lb. × 10-12 reps	2-4 assisted reps
Super pullover	110 lb. × 10-12 reps	2-4 assisted reps
Lateral raise	75 lb. × 10-12 reps	2-4 assisted reps
Biceps curl	65 lb. × 10-12 reps	2-4 assisted reps
Triceps extension	65 lb. × 10-12 reps	2-4 assisted reps
Abdominal curl	105 lb. × 10-12 reps	2-4 assisted reps
Low back extension	115 lb. × 10-12 reps	no post-fatigue reps
Neck flexion	75 lb. × 10-12 reps	no post-fatigue reps
Neck extension	60 lb. × 10-12 reps	no post-fatigue reps

Table 12.3 Sample High-Intensity Strength Training Protocol Using Pre-Exhaustion Training for Major Muscle Groups

Exercise	First (rotary) exercise resistance and repetitions	Second (linear) exercise resistance and repetitions
Leg extension	100 lb. × 8-10 reps	
Leg press		180 lb. × 4-5 reps
Leg curl	80 lb. × 8-10 reps	
Leg press		150 lb. × 4-5 reps
Chest cross	90 lb. × 8-10 reps	
Chest press		140 lb. × 4-5 reps
Pullover	110 lb. × 8-10 reps	
Compound row		150 lb. × 4-5 reps
Lateral raise	75 lb. × 8-10 reps	
Overhead press		100 lb. × 4-5 reps
Biceps curl	65 lb. × 8-10 reps	
Weight-assisted chin-up		40 lb. × 4-5 reps
Triceps extension	65 lb. × 8-10 reps	
Weight-assisted bar dip		40 lb. × 4-5 reps

Table 12.4 Sample High-Intensity Strength Training Protocol Using Slow-Positive Training for Lower Body Exercises and Slow-Negative Training for Upper Body Exercises

Exercise	Resistance and repetitions	Lifting speed (sec.)	Lowering speed (sec.)
Leg extension	80 lb. × 4-6 reps	10	4
Seated leg curl	70 lb. × 4-6 reps	10	4
Leg press	175 lb. × 4-6 reps	10	4
Chest press	130 lb. × 4-6 reps	4	10
Lat pulldown	145 lb. × 4-6 reps	4	10
Overhead press	90 lb. × 4-6 reps	4	10
Biceps curl	55 lb. × 4-6 reps	4	10
Triceps extension	55 lb. × 4-6 reps	4	10
Abdominal curl	95 lb. × 4-6 reps	4	10
Low back extension	100 lb. × 4-6 reps	4	10
Neck flexion	65 lb. × 4-6 reps	4	10
Neck extension	50 lb. × 4-6 reps	4	10

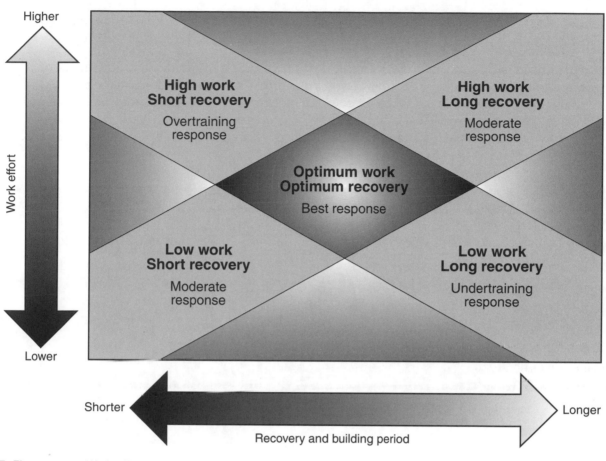

■ **Figure 12.1** Work effort and recovery period.

Advanced Endurance Training

In contrast to strength training, increasing the exercise duration may enhance your endurance development. Just be careful to increase the training time gradually and avoid overtraining. Most authorities recommend the 10 percent rule for increasing your endurance exercise sessions. That is, after the initial conditioning stage (about one month), you should add only 10 percent more training time each week. For example, if at present you are cycling for 30 minutes a session, you should not increase the training time more than 3 minutes a session each week.

Change Training Activities

Like strength training, changing the exercise activities may benefit you both physiologically and psychologically. Different endurance activities involve different muscles but generate similar cardiovascular responses. For example, if you are not advancing in your cycling exercise, switch to another aerobic activity, such as jogging, stepping, or rowing. If you prefer doing a single activity each workout, stay with the new exercise at least one month to allow your body to adapt to the demands of that activity.

You may also change exercises within a given endurance training session as long as you maintain reasonable workout consistency. Cross-training enables you to attain a high cardiovascular effort while working different muscle groups. For example, a 30-minute cross-training session could be divided into 10 minutes of stepping, 10 minutes of recumbent cycling, and 10 minutes of rowing. In this way, you emphasize the front thigh muscles, then the rear thigh muscles, then the upper and lower body muscles. Of course, the heart is pumping hard throughout every phase of the cross-training workout. Program 12.1 shows a sample cross-training session for advanced endurance training.

PROGRAM 12.1   Sample Cross-Training Exercise Combinations

Time[a] (min.)	Activity	Percent max. heart rate
5	Warm-up cycling	50-60
10	Upright cycling	75
10	Treadmill jogging	75
10	Rowing	75
5	Cool-down treadmill walking	50-60

[a]Total workout time = 40 min.

Increase Training Demands

Although steady pace exercise offers a productive approach to endurance development, your cardiovascular system may eventually become accustomed to the same training effort. Interval training is an effective means of increasing the workout demands without increasing the exercise duration.

Consider a 32-minute cycling session that includes a 4-minute warm-up, a 4-minute cool-down, and 24 minutes of moderate-effort endurance training (about 75 percent of maximum heart rate). Now divide the 24-minute conditioning session into six intervals of 4 minutes each. Perform the first, third, and fifth interval at a higher effort level (about 85 percent of maximum heart rate) and do the second, fourth, and sixth interval at a lower effort level (about 65 percent of maximum heart rate). Although the average heart rate response is similar to steady pace exercise, this workout requires a harder training effort and produces a better conditioning effect.

You may redesign your interval training program in a variety of ways to ensure progressive cardiovascular development. For example, you may gradually increase the length of the higher-effort intervals or gradually decrease the length of the lower-effort intervals. As your cardiovascular fitness improves, you can increase your training level for both the higher-effort and lower-effort intervals. The key to advanced interval training is doing three or more challenging rounds of aerobic exercise during each endurance workout. Program 12.2 shows a sample interval training session for advanced endurance training.

PROGRAM 12.2   Sample Interval Training Session

30-min. recumbent cycling workout

Time (min.)	Activity	Percent max. heart rate
4	Warm-up cycling	50-60
4	Higher-effort cycling	85
3	Lower-effort cycling	65
4	Higher-effort cycling	85
3	Lower-effort cycling	65
4	Higher-effort cycling	85
3	Lower-effort cycling	65
4	Cool-down cycling	50-60

Summary

At some point in your exercise program, you will experience a fitness plateau. You need not train harder or progress further if you are satisfied with your current physical condition. If you like your standard exercise routine, simply continue your training program and you will maintain your present fitness level. If you prefer variety, then periodically change your exercises and your training program. In any case, you need not do advanced workouts unless you want to.

If your progress levels off before you reach your fitness goals, however, advanced training procedures should be helpful. Just remember that everyone has different genetic potential for physical performance, so advanced training must be approached sensibly.

Strength plateaus respond well to different training exercises and varied training programs and procedures. Increasing the number of training sets may be productive, but you must be careful to avoid overtraining. A more efficient advanced training approach is to increase the exercise intensity, which may be done by extending the exercise set (breakdown or assisted training), by extending the exercise repetition (slow training), or by performing two successive exercises for the target muscles (pre-exhaustion training). High-intensity training programs are effective for overcoming strength plateaus and increasing muscular fitness. But because of the greater demands and longer recovery period, you should limit high-intensity training to two exercise sessions a week.

To overcome endurance plateaus, you may change the exercise activity or do cross-training. Like strength training, however, further fitness improvements may require more demanding exercise sessions. Interval training is an excellent way to increase the exercise effort without lengthening the exercise time. Training with higher- and lower-effort intervals creates a more challenging exercise program and enhances your cardiovascular fitness. Just be sure to alternate your interval workouts with steady pace sessions to maintain a balanced training program.

References

Chapter 1

1. Centers for Disease Control. 1989. Physical activity, physical fitness, and health: Time to act. *JAMA* 262: 2437.

2. Campbell, W., M. Crim, V. Young, and W. Evans. 1994. Increased energy requirements and changes in body composition with resistance training in older adults. *American Journal of Clinical Nutrition* 60: 167-175.

3. Westcott, W. 1995. *Strength fitness: Physiological principles and training techniques*. 4th ed. Dubuque, IA: Brown and Benchmark.

4. Frontera, W., C. Meredith, K. O'Reilly et al. 1988. Strength conditioning in older men: Skeletal muscle hypertrophy and improved function. *Journal of Applied Physiology* 64 (3): 1038-1044.

5. Fiatarone, M., E. O'Neill, N. Ryan et al. 1994. Exercise training and nutritional supplementation for physical frailty in very elderly people. *The New England Journal of Medicine* 330 (25): 1169-1175.

6. Faigenbaum, A., L. Zaichkowsky, W. Westcott et al. 1993. The effects of a twice-a-week strength training program on children. *Pediatric Exercise Science* 5: 339-346.

7. Westcott, W. 1994. Studies show significant gains in young muscles. *Nautilus* 3: 2, 6-7.

8. ——. 1995. Women vs. men: Are women really the weaker sex? *Nautilus* 4 (4): 3-5.

9. Sharkey, B.J. 1990. *Physiology of fitness*. 3d ed. Champaign, IL: Human Kinetics.

10. Wilmore, J.H., and D.L. Costill. 1994. *Physiology of sport and exercise*. Champaign, IL: Human Kinetics.

11. Halloszy, J.O. 1967. Biomechanical adaptations in muscle: Effects of exercise on mitochondrial oxygen uptake and respiratory enzyme activity in skeletal muscle. *Journal of Biological Chemistry* 242: 2278-2282.

12. *University of California at Berkeley Wellness Letter*. 1995. Young at 70. 11 (May): 2-3.

Chapter 2

1. Westcott, W. 1995. *Strength fitness: Physiological principles and training techniques*. 4th Ed. Dubuque, IA: Brown and Benchmark.

2. Faigenbaum, A., L. Zaichkowsky, W. Westcott et al. 1992. Effects of twice per week strength training program on children. Paper presented at the annual meeting of the New England Chapter of American College of Sports Medicine, 12 November, at Boxborough, Massachusetts.

3. Westcott, W. 1995. Keeping fit. *Nautilus* 4 (2): 5-7.

4. Westcott, W., and Guy, J. 1996. A physical evolution: Sedentary adults see marked improvements in as little as two days a week. *IDEA Today* 14 (9): 58-65.

5. Darden, E. 1987. *The Nautilus diet*. Boston: Little, Brown & Company.

6. Sheridan, S., T. Dohmeier, and J. Cleland. 1995. Effect of biometrics on body composition, strength, and blood lipid changes in middle age women. *Medicine and Science in Sports and Exercise* 27 (5): S140 Supplement.

7. Westcott, W. 1993. Weight gain and weight loss. *Nautilus* 3 (1): 8-9.

8. Evans, W., I. Rosenberg. 1992. *Biomarkers.* New York: Simon & Schuster.

9. Keyes, A., H.L. Taylor, and F. Grande. 1973. Basal metabolism and age of adult man. *Metabolism* 22: 579-587.

10. Melby, C., C. Scholl, G. Edwards et al. 1993. Effect of acute resistance exercise on postexercise energy expenditure and resting metabolic rate. *Journal of Applied Physiology* 75 (4): 1847-1853.

11. Campbell, W., M. Crim, V. Young, and W. Evans. 1994. Increased energy requirements and changes in body composition with resistance training in older adults. *American Journal of Clinical Nutrition* 60: 167-175.

12. Pratley, R., B. Nickolas, M. Rubin; J. Miller, A. Smith, M. Smith; B. Hurley, and A. Goldberg. 1994. Strength training increases resting metabolic rate and norepinephrine levels in healthy 50- to 65-year-old men. *Journal of Applied Physiology* 76: 133-137.

13. Drayoritch, P., and W. Westcott. 1999. *Complete conditioning for golf.* Champaign, IL: Human Kinetics.

14. Risch, S., N. Nowell, M. Pollock et al. 1993. Lumbar strengthening in chronic low back pain patients. *Spine* 18: 232-238.

15. Menkes, A., S. Mazel, A. Redmond et al. 1993. Strength training increases regional bone mineral density and bone remodeling in middle-aged and older men. *Journal of Applied Physiology* 74: 2478-2484.

16. Hurley, B. 1994. Does strength training improve health status? *Strength and Conditioning Journal* 16: 7-13.

17. Koffler, K., A. Menkes, A. Redmond et al. 1992. Strength training accelerates gastrointestinal transit in middle-aged and older men. *Medicine and Science in Sports and Exercise* 24: 415-419.

18. Stone, M., D. Blessing, R. Byrd et al. 1982. Physiological effects of a short term resistive training program on middle-aged untrained men. *National Strength and Conditioning Association Journal* 4: 16-20.

19. Hurley, B., J. Hagberg, A. Goldberg et al. 1988. Resistance training can reduce coronary risk factors without altering $\dot{V}O_2$max or percent body fat. *Medicine and Science in Sports and Exercise* 20: 150-154.

20. *Tufts University Diet and Nutrition Letter.* 1994. Never too late to build up your muscle. 12 (September): 6-7.

21. Westcott, W. 1993. Strength training and blood pressure response. *Nautilus* 2 (4): 8-9.

22. Harris, K., and R. Holly. 1987. Physiological response to circuit weight training in borderline hypertensive subjects. *Medicine and Science in Sports and Exercise* 19: 246-252.

23. Sing, N., K. Clements, and M. Fiatorone. 1997. A randomized controlled trial of progressive resistance training in depressed elders. *Journal of Gerontology* 52A (1): M27-M35.

24. Braith, R., J. Graves, M. Pollock et al. 1989. Comparison of two versus three days per week of variable resistance training during 10 and 18 week programs. *International Journal of Sports Medicine* 10: 450-454.

25. American College of Sports Medicine. 1990. The recommended quantity and quality of exercise for developing and maintaining cardiorespiratory and muscular fitness in healthy adults. *Medicine and Science in Sports and Exercise* 22: 265-274.

26. Faigenbaum, M., and M. Pollock. 1999. Prescription of resistance training for health and disease. *Medicine and Science in Sports and Exercise* 31 (1): 38-45.

27. Westcott, W., K. Greenberger, and D. Milius. 1989. Strength training research: Sets and repetitions. *Scholastic Coach* 58: 98-100.

28. Starkey, D., M. Welsch, M. Pollock et al. 1994. Equivalent improvement in strength following high intensity, low and high volume training. Paper presented at the annual meeting of the American College of Sports Medicine, 2 June, at Indianapolis, Indiana.

29. Westcott, W. 1993. How many repetitions? *Nautilus* 2 (3): 6-7.

30. ———. 1994. Exercise speed and strength development. *American Fitness Quarterly* 13 (3): 20-21.

31. Jones, A., M. Pollock, J. Graves et al. 1988. *Safe, specific testing and rehabilitative exercise for the muscles of the lumbar spine.* Santa Barbara, CA: Sequoia Communications.

32. Risch, S., N. Nowell, M. Pollock et al. 1993. Lumbar strengthening in chronic low back pain patients. *Spine* 18: 232-238.

33. Westcott, W., and R. La Rosa Loud. 1999. Strength, stretch and stamina. *Fitness Management* 15 (6): 44-45.

34. Westcott, W., and R. La Rosa Loud. 2000. Stretching for strength. *Fitness Management* 16 (7): 44-46.

35. Westcott, W., M. Richards, G. Rein, and D. Califano. (In press). Strength training elderly nursing home patients. *Newsletter of the American Senior Fitness Association.*

36. Westcott, W. 1994. High intensity strength training. *Nautilus* 4 (1): 5-8.

Chapter 5

1. Westcott, W. 1997. Strength training 201. *Fitness Management* 13 (7): 33-35.

2. Westcott, W. 1998. High intensities improve body composition. *ACE Certified News* 4 (2): 1-3.

3. Westcott, W., R. Winett, E. Anderson, J. Wojcik, R. Loud, E. Cleggett, and S. Glover. 2001. Effects of regular and slow speed resistance training on muscle strength. *Journal of Sports Medicine and Physical Fitness* 41: 154-158.

4. Westcott, W. 1995. High-intensity strength training. *IDEA Personal Trainer* 6: 7,9.

5. Westcott, W., J. Annesi, T. D'Arpino, and B. Burak. 2001. Boot camp vs. high-intensity training. *Fitness Management* 17 (7): 46-49.

Chapter 6

1. *Harvard Heart Letter.* 1995. Data debunk myths about heart disease. 5 (June): 1-3.

2. Powell, K.E., P.D. Thompson, C.J. Caspersen et al. 1987. Physical activity and the incidence of coronary heart disease. *Annual Reviews in Public Health* 8: 253-287.

3. Caspersen, C.J. 1987. Physical inactivity and coronary heart disease. *The Physician and Sportsmedicine* 15: 43-44.

4. Peters, R.K., L.D. Cady, Jr., D.P. Bischoff et al. 1983. Physical fitness and subsequent myocardial infarction in healthy workers. *JAMA* 249: 3052-3056.

5. Blair, S.N., H.W. Kohl, III, D.G. Paffenbarger, Jr. et al. 1989. Physical fitness and all-cause mortality: A prospective study of healthy men and women. *JAMA* 262: 2395-2401.

6. American College of Sports Medicine. 1990. The recommended quantity and quality of exercise for developing and maintaining cardiorespiratory and muscular fitness in healthy adults. *Medicine and Science in Sports and Exercise* 22: 265-274.

7. Fox, S.M., J.P. Naughton, and P.A. Gorman. 1972. Physical activity and cardiovascular health. *Modern Concepts of Cardiovascular Health* 41: 20.

8. Harris, K.A., and R.G. Holly. 1987. Physiological response to circuit weight training in borderline hypertensive subjects. *Medicine and Science in Sports and Exercise* 19: 246-252.

9. Westcott, W. 1993. Strength training and blood pressure response. *Nautilus* 2 (Fall): 8-9.

10. Seals, D.R., and J.M. Hagberg. 1984. The effect of exercise training on human hypertension: A review. *Medicine and Science in Sports and Exercise* 16: 207-215.

11. Goldberg, L., and D.L. Elliot. 1985. The effect of physical activity on lipid and lipoprotein levels. *Medical Clinics of North America* 69: 41-55.

12. Pomerleau, O., H. Scherzer, N. Grunberg et al. 1987. The effects of acute exercise on subsequent cigarette smoking. *Journal of Behavioral Medicine* 10: 117-127.

13. *Tufts University Diet and Nutrition Letter.* 1994. To diet or not? The experts battle it out. 12 (October): 3-6.

14. Zuti, W.B., and L. Golding. 1976. Comparing diet and exercise as weight reduction tools. *The Physician and Sportsmedicine* 4: 59-62.

15. Rippe, J.M. 1992. *The exercise exchange program.* New York: Simon & Schuster.

16. Westcott, W. 1993. Weight gain and weight loss. *Nautilus* 3 (Winter): 8-9.

17. Wilmore, J.H., and D.L. Costill. 1994. *Physiology of sport and exercise.* Champaign, IL: Human Kinetics.

18. Sharkey, B.J. 1990. *Physiology of fitness.* 3d ed. Champaign, IL: Human Kinetics.

19. Pollock, M.L., L.R. Gettman, M.D. Milesis et al. 1977. Effects of frequency and duration of training on attrition and incidence of injury. *Medicine and Science in Sports* 9: 31-36.

20. Porcari, J.P. 1994. Fat-burning exercise: Fit or farce. *Fitness Management* 10: 40-41.

Chapter 7

1. Westcott, W. 1991. Comparison of upright and recumbent cycling exercise. *American Fitness Quarterly* 10 (October): 36-38.

2. ———. 1995. From the world of research: The skate machine. *American Fitness Quarterly* 13: 20-21.

Chapter 8

1. Messier, S., and M. Dill. 1985. Alterations in strength and maximal oxygen update consequent to Nautilus circuit weight training. *Research Quarterly for Exercise and Sport* 56 (4): 345-351.

2. Gettman, L., P. Ward, and R. Hagan. 1982. A comparison of combined running and weight training with circuit weight training. *Medicine and Science in Sports and Exercise* 14 (3): 229-234.

Chapter 11

1. Westcott, W. 1986. Integration of strength, endurance and skill training. *Scholastic Coach* 55 (May-June): 74.

2. ———. 1995. *Strength fitness: Physiological principles and training techniques.* 4th Ed. Dubuque, IA: Brown and Benchmark.

3. Westcott, W., and R. La Rosa Loud. 1999. Strength, stretch and stamina. *Fitness Management* 115 (6): 44-45.

4. McCarthy, J., J. Agre, B. Graf et al. 1995. Compatibility of adaptive responses with combining strength and endurance training. *Medicine and Science in Sports and Exercise* 273: 429-436.

5. Westcott, W., and R. La Rosa Loud. 2000. Stretching for strength. *Fitness Management* 16 (7): 44-46.

6. Westcott, W. 1987. *Building strength at the YMCA.* Champaign, IL: Human Kinetics.

Index

Note: The italicized *f* and *t* following page numbers refer to figures and tables, respectively.

About the Author

Wayne L. Westcott, PhD, CSCS, is fitness research director at the South Shore YMCA in Quincy, Massachusetts. With more than 35 years in strength training as an athlete, coach, teacher, professor, researcher, writer, and speaker, Westcott is recognized as a leading authority on fitness. He has served as a strength training consultant for numerous national organizations and programs, including Nautilus, the President's Council on Physical Fitness and Sports, the National School Fitness Foundation, the International Association of Fitness Professionals, the American Council on Exercise, the YMCA of the USA, and the National Youth Sports Safety Foundation. He has also served as trainer for U.S. Navy fitness leaders. Westcott has received numerous awards, including five National Fitness Profession Leadership Awards, the Governor's Council Lifetime Achievement Award, the IDEA Lifetime Achievement Award, and the President's Council Healthy American Fitness Leader Award.

Westcott has authored or coauthored 15 other books on strength training, including *Strength Training Past 50*, *Strength Training for Seniors*, *Complete Conditioning for Golf*, and *Strength and Power for Young Athletes*. In addition, he has served on the editorial boards of *Prevention*, *Shape*, *Men's Health*, *Fitness*, *Club Industry*, *American Fitness Quarterly*, and *Nautilus*.

Westcott lives in Abington, Massachusetts, with his wife, Claudia.